J

Praise for

THE REFORMATION 500 YEARS LATER

"Benjamin Wiker has written a highly compelling, culturally rich book, studded with historical ironies. Yes, there is the power of ideas themselves and they have consequences, but *how* they came to power and in whose interests are also indispensable parts of the story. Wiker reveals the way the secular revolution used the Reformation to further its aim of extinguishing Catholics and Protestants alike. Without gainsaying the profound differences between Protestantism and Catholicism, he also shows the grounds on which they urgently need to come together so that Christianity itself can survive the onslaughts against it from the rabid secularism and militant Islam of our times."

—**Robert R. Reilly,** special assistant to Ronald Reagan and author of *The Closing of the Muslim Mind* and *Making Gay Okay*

"While simplicity is often sought to calm the mind, it rarely offers an accurate picture of real life. Dr. Ben Wiker complicates easy and simplistic understandings of the five-hundred-year-old Reformation with facts about the richly complicated and interwoven factors underlying that history. Important factors of early nationalism, Renaissance paganism and atheism, Turkish Islamic imperialism, the saintly and sinful popes, and the origins of ideas like 'Scripture alone' and the supremacy of the state over the church interacted and brought much havoc. Wiker tells this story resolutely, honestly, and well. This is a great read for the five-hundredth anniversary of the Reformation."

—**Fr. Mitch Pacwa, S.J.,** founder and president of Ignatius Productions and EWTN television and radio host

"I first became aware of Ben Wiker when, some years ago, I was browsing the new releases at a Barnes & Noble. Seeing his cleverly titled romp *10 Books That Screwed Up the World*, I picked it up and thumbed its pages expecting to find that his list included all the books that I held dear, the Holy Bible chief among them. I instead found something quite different. Indeed, had I scribbled a list of odious books on a napkin and then compared it to Wiker's table of contents, I might have scored 7/10. Skimming a page or two, I decided to buy the book and hurried home to read it. There I discovered a scholar with a first-rate mind whose often witty, always accessible prose made for delightful reading.

"These days I know the man behind the book. Ben is not only a colleague-at-large, he is my dear friend. In *The Reformation 500 Years Later* he has written his best, and certainly his timeliest, book. It is neither an air-brushed account of Catholic Church history, nor is it an assault on events celebrated by Protestants in this, the quincentennial of the Protestant Reformation. It is, rather, an honest Catholic's appraisal of the factors contributing to that watershed event and the ramifications of it. More importantly, Ben has not written a history in the traditional sense; he has written a book on current events that looks in the rearview mirror for clues. *The Reformation 500 Years Later* will be enjoyed by both Catholics and Protestants alike and, if Ben succeeds in his noble aim, they will find a common cause."

—**Larry Taunton,** founder and executive director of Fixed Point Foundation and author of *The Grace Effect*

The Reformation 500 Years Later

THE
REFORMATION
500 YEARS LATER

12 THINGS YOU NEED
TO KNOW

BENJAMIN WIKER

REGNERY
HISTORY

Regnery History™ is a trademark of Salem Communications Holding Corporation; Regnery® is a registered trademark of Salem Communications Holding Corporation

Scriptures taken from the Holy Bible, New International Version®, NIV®. Copyright © 1973, 1978, 1984, 2011 by Biblica, Inc.™ Used by permission of Zondervan. All rights reserved worldwide. www.Zondervan.com. The "NIV" and "New International Version" are trademarks registered in the United States Patent and Trademark Office by Biblica, Inc.™

Cataloging-in-Publication data on file with the Library of Congress

ISBN 978-1-62157-670-9
e-book ISBN 978-1-62157-706-5

Published in the United States by
Regnery History
An imprint of Regnery Publishing
A Division of Salem Media Group
300 New Jersey Ave NW
Washington, DC 20001
www.RegneryHistory.com

Manufactured in the United States of America

10 9 8 7 6 5 4 3 2 1

Books are available in quantity for promotional or premium use. For information on discounts and terms, please visit our website: www.Regnery.com.

Distributed to the trade by
Perseus Distribution
www.perseusdistribution.com

*To my great Evangelical friend in Christ,
Larry Taunton, whose Christian courage, intelligence,
and faith are such a deep inspiration*

Contents

WHY THE REFORMATION IS COMING TO AN END, BUT CHRISTIANITY (MOST PROBABLY) IS NOT

T he first thing to understand about the Reformation is that after five hundred years it is coming to an end. If we don't understand that essential fact, then we'll be confused about its beginning, which commenced when Martin Luther allegedly nailed his *Ninety-Five Theses* to the Wittenberg Castle Church door on October 31, 1517. (He actually didn't nail them but mailed them, as we'll soon enough discover.)

The Reformation is coming to an end because Christians are focused increasingly on what unites them, largely because of mounting persecution. J. R. R. Tolkien's classic, *The Lord of the Rings*, offers a good analogy here. The dwarves and elves have been fighting with each other for generations. Faced with a common foe bent on destroying them both (Sauron and his army of orcs), the dwarves and elves form a deep friendship forged in the battles to keep Middle Earth from falling to the powers of darkness.

I will not say who are the elves and who are the dwarves—the fictional analogy is not that exact. (Although, when I, a Catholic, get together with my good Evangelical friend Larry Taunton who is well over six feet, it's certain that central casting would peg me as the dwarf.) But elves and dwarves aside, it's clear that the malignance of those bent on destroying Christians over the last century has created common and commonly admired heroes. What Catholic could not admire the great Lutheran martyr Dietrich Bonhoeffer, who was executed at the concentration camp at Flossenbürg on April 9, 1945? What Protestant could not admire St. Maximilian Kolbe, who was executed at Auschwitz on August 14, 1941?

Many true and deep ecumenical friendships have also been nurtured among those gathered to protest the holocaust of abortion, or to work against the federal government's attempt to impose gay marriage or transgender bathroom policies, or to fight the culture of death's romance with eugenics and euthanasia, or to wage a common counteroffensive against the increasing vulgarity of a pornographied culture, or to watch with increasing horror as Christians are martyred in ever greater numbers around the globe.

We may think that Christian martyrs are found primarily in the ancient world, during the persecution by the pagan Roman state, but the greatest century for martyrdom is the twentieth, and who knows if the twenty-first might surpass it.[1] More than half of the Christians martyred in the two-thousand-year history of Christianity lost their lives in the twentieth century (about forty-five million).[2]

Many of these Christians were among the hundred million slaughtered by Communism—that is, by atheist states like the Soviet Union and Red China. But the turn into the twenty-first century didn't bring a decrease in carnage. It is estimated that the rate of slaughter continues to be about a hundred thousand Christians per year, or "eleven Christians killed every hour, every day," notes journalist John Allen. "That is a truly ecumenical scourge, in the sense that it afflicts evangelicals, mainline Protestants, Anglicans, Orthodox, Catholics, and Pentecostals alike. All denominations have their martyrs, and all are more or less equally at risk."[3]

The evangelical missionary and persecution-watch organization Open Doors has ranked the most dangerous places for a Christian to live today.[4] The list of top ten places is instructive if we include in parentheses who is doing the persecuting. The honor of the worst goes to North Korea (Communists), then Somalia (Muslims), Afghanistan (Muslims), Pakistan (Muslims), Sudan (Muslims), Syria (Muslims), Iraq (Muslims), Iran (Muslims), Yemen (Muslims), and Eritrea (leftist nationalist tyranny by the People's Front for Democracy and Justice).

A glance at the next ten worst underlines an obvious trend: Libya (Muslims), Nigeria (Muslims), Maldives (Muslims), Saudi Arabia (Muslims), India (Hindus), Uzbekistan (Muslims), Vietnam (Communists and Buddhists), Kenya (Muslims), Turkmenistan (Muslims), and Qatar (Muslims).

Radical Islam is the most potent source of anti-Christian persecution. But unsurprisingly, the remaining Communist regimes (China, North Korea, Vietnam, Laos, and Cuba) still routinely persecute Christians, even if they don't martyr them on a twentieth century scale.[5] Christians are also easy targets of nationalist regimes, sometimes under brutal military rule, sometimes engaging in ethnic warfare, as in the Democratic Republic of the Congo and Myanmar (Burma).

Predictably, the secular press largely ignores the persecution of Christians today, just as it ignored it when perpetrated by Communists in the twentieth century. Western Christians, however, are slowly but surely becoming more and more aware of the worldwide threats. So, even with our differences, we Christians are being driven together by persecution and martyrdom.

In the United States, it isn't outright martyrdom that Christians experience, but the lesser modes of persecution by the dominant, decaying, secularized culture. Protestants and Catholics alike lament the prevalence of divorce and cohabitation because both believe that marriage is a holy, God-ordained institution, even if they don't agree on whether it is a sacrament. Both fight side by side for religious freedom, the protection of the right to worship, and the right to have a Christian moral understanding inform our common political life, even with our differences in the way we worship and the finer lines of what we believe.

Catholics and Protestants have grown together to act as a counterforce against aggressive secularism at home and persecution abroad. More and more, we Christians feel as if we are being backed into a single great castle—to borrow from Tolkien again, as in the battle of Helm's Deep. There, as we rub shoulders, make common plans, eat common meals, and fight side by side against the seemingly endless tide of destroyers, the old controversies and old wounds fade by comparison, and a fresh charity prevails.

Ironically, there is also a drawing together of serious, orthodox Christians when faced with heterodoxy within their own Church. An orthodox Catholic and orthodox Lutheran or an orthodox Presbyterian have much more in common, theologically, than an orthodox and liberal Catholic, an orthodox and liberal Lutheran, or an orthodox and liberal Presbyterian. Liberalism represents a common foe seeking to erode the central doctrinal integrity that defines Christianity, replacing the Nicene Creed's crisp, straight lines about the Holy Trinity and the economy of salvation, with the Nice Creed's soft, wavy mixture of pop psychology and political correctness.

I am inclined to think all of this is an act of Providence, or better, that God is patiently bringing a great good out of evident evils. However that may be, it's clear that Christianity itself is under attack, from without and from within, and in facing these common threats, true Christians realize that for Christianity to survive at all (to borrow Benjamin Franklin's famous words, spoken in another context), "We must, indeed, all hang together, or most assuredly we shall all hang separately."

In that spirit, Protestants and Catholics are coming together in their fundamental understanding of the Christian faith. In this happy development too, the Reformation is coming to an end.

Five hundred years ago, Martin Luther and other Protestant reformers complained that the Catholic Church neglected Holy Scripture, and instead focused its energies almost entirely on self-maintenance of the ecclesiastical hierarchy, protecting itself from criticism by keeping the Bible in Latin and out of the hands of the laity.

What would Martin Luther think of reading the following from *Dei Verbum*, promulgated by Pope Paul VI on November 18, 1965?

> Easy access to Sacred Scripture should be provided for all the Christian faithful. That is why the Church from

the very beginning accepted as her own that very ancient Greek translation of the Old Testament which is called the Septuagint; and she has always given a place of honor to other Eastern translations and Latin ones, especially the Latin translation known as the vulgate. But since the word of God should be accessible at all times, the Church by her authority and with maternal concern sees to it that suitable and correct translations are made into different languages, especially from the original texts of the sacred books. And should the opportunity arise and the Church authorities approve, if these translations are produced in cooperation with the separated brethren as well, all Christians will be able to use them.[6]

Or what would Martin Luther think today if he walked into a Catholic Mass and found that the Catholic Church cycles through the Bible on a three-year rotation, the priest or lector reading to the laity (in their own language) selections from the Old Testament, the Letters of St. Paul, and the Gospels?

As is well known, one of the biggest disputes arising in the Reformation was over the way that Christians were saved, Luther famously asserting that works were to no avail because Christians had to be justified by faith alone. What would he think of the *Joint Declaration on the Doctrine of Justification* by the Lutheran World Federation and the Catholic Church issued in 1999?[7] In it, both sides officially agree that

on the basis of their dialogue the subscribing Lutheran churches and the Roman Catholic Church are now able to articulate a common understanding of our justification by God's grace through faith in Christ. It does not cover all that either church teaches about justification; it does encompass a consensus on basic truths of the doctrine of justification and shows that the remaining differences in its explication are no longer the occasion for doctrinal condemnations.[8]

The *Joint Declaration* further notes

that in overcoming the earlier controversial questions and doctrinal condemnations, the churches neither take the condemnations lightly nor do they disavow their own past. On the contrary, this Declaration is shaped by the conviction that in their respective histories our churches have come to new insights. Developments have taken place which not only make possible, but also require the churches to examine the divisive questions and condemnations and see them in a new light.[9]

In other words, current ecumenical efforts are real efforts to heal on the deepest levels, not just a "forgive and forget, and let's bury all this doctrinal nonsense and yodel *Kumbaya*." Yet, there is recognition on both sides that, perhaps, in the heat of battle, the case on one's own side was overstated, and the valid points on the other side were barely heard or misunderstood.

On the Protestant side, I don't know of many Protestants who are proud of the splintering of Christianity into a multitude of different denominations, and so they have a greater appreciation for the unity of the Catholic Church.

Even more, many Protestants have expressed their admiration for a single, unifying head of the Church, based in their experience of watching the unfolding of the amazing pontificate of St. John Paul II. A half a millennium ago, it was easy to think of the reprehensible and irreligious Pope Alexander VI (1492–1503) as "the whore of Babylon," but that oft-used Reformation epithet is woefully out of place in regard to someone as saintly as John Paul II. And Protestants know that.

Or, to take one more instance, many Protestants appreciate the comprehensiveness and logical unity of Catholic moral doctrine, and even more, of an authoritative hierarchy that can make moral pronouncements and enforce them among the faithful. As we enter into a time where new moral challenges arise almost daily from ambiguous technological advances in genetic and reproductive manipulation, as well as from unambiguous assaults on the integrity of human sexuality, this kind of moral authority is welcome to any Christian.

On the Catholic side again, I know of more than a few Catholics who admire the Anglican liturgy, or the Presbyterian emphasis on the sermon, or the political unity of Evangelical voters that would amount to a transformative Christianizing of our politics if it was matched by a similar unity among Catholic voters.

Now I must make clear, in saying that the Reformation is coming to an end, I am not making exact predictions that by such and such a date all Christians will be united in one comprehensive Christian Church. That would be presumptuous on my part, as if I had some special mystical insight into the ways of Divine Providence.

Nor will the end of the Reformation come about automatically or easily. It will be difficult, and a great part of that difficulty will be clearing up five hundred years of confusion about what really happened in the Reformation, and what the implications were. Too much of our understanding of the Reformation focuses solely on the theological disagreements, too little on the political and intellectual context that exacerbated and magnified those disagreements, which did as much, if not more, to cause a series of fractures in the Body of Christ rather than a healing, unifying reform.

Please do not misunderstand this assertion. The theological disagreements were (and still are) important and the need for reform was acute, but there were other, external influences and actors who used the disagreements and the earnest desire to reform for their own purposes. To name two of the many we'll be covering in this book: rulers who wanted to use Christians as pawns in their political ambitions, and a new brand of secular philosophers whose desire to rid the world of Christianity brought them to use a "divide and conquer" strategy, pitting Protestant against Catholic.

As you may have already guessed, my goal is not to provide yet another basic history of the Reformation—there are already enough out there, and we didn't have to wait until the quincentennial of Luther's *Ninety-Five Theses*. Rather, I'm hoping to show readers the broader, deeper reasons why the Reformation happened (and consequently, why it might not have happened), what other movements were already at work trying to destroy Christianity even before the Reformation (and how they used the Reformation for their purposes), the mistakes that both Catholics and Protestants made, and the ambiguities that most histories of the Reformation ignore.

In all this, my hope is that *all* Christians more deeply understand that, despite our best and worst efforts, God is providentially guiding us all toward an ever more profound unity as the One Body of Christ. The world desperately needs the light of Jesus Christ in these ever-darker times. The fate of Christianity is the fate of the world. If that Light should flicker out, there is no other. I offer this book in hopes that it may, by the Grace of God, help in some small way to rekindle the flame in this, the twenty-first century of Christianity, so that it may not be the last. The Reformation is ending, but Christianity must not.

As the title says, I'm offering twelve things you need to know about the Reformation, the first of which we have covered in this chapter. Each of them contributes to a deeper understanding of the Reformation, and the situation of all Christians five hundred years later.

One thing that will become very clear is how much we need to know about what happened in the centuries before Luther to understand what happened in the Reformation and the centuries that follow it. For that very reason, there will be more than a few chapters before we finally turn to a deeper consideration of Luther himself.

Given this approach, it will be helpful if readers have a quick "score card" of the 1500s, the defining century of the Reformation, just to have the basic "players" in mind. The important details will be filled in at the appropriate places in later chapters.

During the 1500s, all the major lines of Protestantism would arise and take definitive form: Lutherans, the eponymous followers of Martin Luther (1483–1546); the Zwinglians, after Huldrych Zwingli (1484–1531) who ended up half-way between the Anabaptists and later Calvinists; the Reformed, or Calvinists, the followers of John Calvin (1504–1564) who thought Zwinglians and Anabaptists had gone too far and Lutherans not far enough; the Anglicans, at the behest of King Henry VIII (1491–1547) who formed the most obvious form of political religion; and the

Anabaptists, the radical reformers who took Protestant principles to conclusions rejected by Lutherans, Zwinglians, Calvinists, and Anglicans—and even many Anabaptists. (There is no single founder of the Anabaptist movement.)

All the major branches of Protestantism stem from these foundations, either by direct lineage or cross-fertilization. All share a common rejection of the papacy as authoritative, and rest authority instead on the Bible alone (hence the Reformation battle cry, *sola scriptura*), though disagreements over how to interpret the Bible led to Protestantism's many internal divisions.

Luther, for instance, believed that man was redeemed not by any good works but by "faith alone," *sola fide*, and rejected five of the seven sacraments of the Catholic Church (Confirmation, Marriage, Holy Orders, Extreme Unction, and, after some struggle, Penitential Confession). But he affirmed that the Eucharist was real rather than symbolic and that Baptism was necessary for salvation (and even more, that infants should be baptized). Some of Luther's immediate followers accepted his doctrines of *sola scriptura* and *sola fide*, but believed that if Christians are saved by faith alone, then *any* sacraments were a form of crypto—(and corrupt)—Catholicism.

Zwingli and all Anabaptists took this view, and Luther absolutely hated the Anabaptists, believing they (along with Catholics) were satanically inspired.

Calvin, who appeared on the scene after Luther's death, took the side of the Anabaptists in regard to the sacraments, even while despising the more radical Anabaptist disregard of Church structure and discipline and ambivalence about the Nicene Creed, *the* fundamental statement of Christian orthodoxy accepted by both Catholics and Protestants.

The Anglican Church, which was really a nationalized English Church, generally agreed with Luther about the sacraments as couched in a very Catholic liturgical setting, but ended up interpreting them in a way that was palatable to Calvinists and more conservative Anabaptists, thereby creating a broad Church that claimed to be one of three apostolic Churches (Anglican, Catholic, and Orthodox) but that seemed to outsiders like an impossible chimera of mix-and-match Protestantism and Catholicism.

Catholics had their own reform during this century. After much hesitation and prodding, the Church finally called a reform council that had teeth in it, the Council of Trent (1545–1563). Inevitably, if unfortunately, much of the Council's necessary reform was defined *against* Protestantism, (hence the "Counter-Reformation"), because the various Protestant movements had accused the Catholic Church not just of corruption, but of fundamental doctrinal errors.

All these religious differences could not help but to inform and exacerbate already existing political differences. The result was war, both within Protestantism (as in the German Peasants War, 1524–1525) and between Catholicism and Lutheranism, or more accurately, between the Catholic Holy Roman Emperor and some of the Protestant German princes. The first round of the Catholic-Lutheran wars ended in the stalemate of the Peace of Augsburg (1555) which declared that each ruler, Catholic or Lutheran, would decide the religion of his realm (captured in the memorable Latin phrase, *cuius regio, eius religio*, "whose realm, his religion").

In Catholic France, noblemen who wanted to revolt against the king found their justification in Calvinism, which authorized such rebellions. As with the earlier battles between Catholics and Lutherans, this one between the Catholic crown and the Calvinist nobles ended in a stalemate (the Edict of Nantes, 1598), not defined by *cuius regio, eius religio* but the legal toleration of Reformed Churches in the officially Catholic country of France.

Near the end of the century, Nicene orthodoxy began to unravel, in part as a result of the adoption of the principle of *sola scriptura*, most notably with the heterodox ruminations of the Italian Fausto Paolo Sozzini (Latinized as Faustus Socinus, 1539–1604) after whom Socinianism is named. Socinianism was actually a rebirth of the fourth-century heresy of Arianism that proclaimed that Jesus Christ was not divine, and like Arianism it based its case upon Scripture.

There you have it, a quick look at the basics of the 1500s, the defining century of the Reformation. With that as a framework, we may now turn to a deeper consideration of what you really need to know about the Reformation.

CHAPTER TWO

WHY REFORMATIONS WILL BE WITH US TO THE END (BECAUSE THEY HAVE BEEN WITH US FROM THE BEGINNING)

It will seem paradoxical, right after asserting in the last chapter that the Reformation is coming to an end, to claim in this one that reformations will be with us to the end. But understanding that both are equally true is essential to clearing up our confusions about the Reformation (and our own situation today, as well as what we can expect in the future).

Much of the feeling of paradox will be removed by understanding the difference between big "R" and little "r" reformation. The Reformation is capitalized because it is a definite, recognizable, singular historical event, one which famously began in 1517 in Germany. Little "r" reformation, on the other hand, tells us that we are referring indefinitely to a plurality of ongoing attempts at the reformation of Christianity, of which the Reformation is just one.

Putting the Reformation into the context of the endless reformations that have occurred since the beginning of Christianity helps clarify a significant amount of our confusion about what the Reformation really was, especially if we add that the Reformation didn't stop reformations, which have been occurring ceaselessly among both Catholics and all Protestants down to the present day.

We might begin to understand the importance of this clarifying exercise by asking a question: given that there were many reformations in the centuries before and after the time of Luther, how is it that one of those reform movements punctuating the history of Christianity turned into the Reformation?

To answer that question fully is one of the goals of this book. In this chapter, we will focus on the initial clarifying aspect, establishing the fact that the history of the Christian Church *is* the history of constant reform.

Upon some reflection, this fact should not surprise any Christians, given that the Church made the seeming tactical error (granted, at the command of God) of letting human beings in from the start, with all their foibles, confusions, short-sightedness, and sins. As long as this policy continues, and God incorporates fallen man and woman within the Body of Christ, we can expect the future Church to be a mixed bag in need of constant reform.

But this fact is often neglected. While it should not surprise us Christians—I believe there is a doctrine somewhere about original sin—we may not have sufficiently understood, historically, how many reforms there were prior to the Reformation, and where the

Reformation fits, historically and theologically, in that continuum. Would that I had time and space to deal with the countless reform efforts after the Reformation, but that would make this chapter stretch into a book. The number of different Protestant denominations has increased tremendously over the last five centuries, because reform movements within each often result in its further splintering, and these "sub-groups" have their own respective reform movements in turn. So let's stick with the time period leading up to Luther, which will be more than sufficient to make the point about endless reforms.

The Biblical Witness of the Continual Need to Reform

If you or I were among the first Christians we may well have given in to the very human temptation to fudge the truth a bit and hide our family quarrels. Thank God the four Gospel writers and St. Paul did not yield to that temptation—they told the unbecoming truth.

There are several reports from Christians of the first centuries (Bishop Papias of Hierapolis, Irenaeus, Justin Martyr, Clement, and Eusebius) that the Gospel of Mark was written by Mark under the direction of St. Peter. Mark faithfully records the embarrassing dust-ups between Peter and Jesus, including Jesus's rebuking His apostle with the words, "Get behind me, Satan! For you are not on the side of God, but of men," (Mk 8:32–33) and His prediction, despite Peter's protestations of loyalty, that "before the cock crows twice, you will deny me three times" (Mk 14:29–31, 14:66–72).

This was the same apostle (originally named Simon) that Jesus himself renamed "Peter" (meaning "rock," from the Greek *petros*), telling him that "on this rock I will build my church, and the powers of death shall not prevail against it" (Mt 16:18, Jn 1:42).

Whatever one might think about Petrine authority and the papacy, this is admittedly a humble and humbling beginning for one of the Church's chief apostles. And if we trust the ancient authorities about the authorship of the Gospel of Mark, then Peter himself, through Mark, was divinely moved to ensure that we saw him warts and all. With this beginning, we should not be surprised that the crucifixion, death, resurrection, and ascension into heaven of Jesus didn't yield a Church chock-full of saints without friction and struggle. Instead, the Bible reports holiness and faithfulness *and* the need for reform among its members straight from the get-go.

In the Acts of the Apostles, we find Peter, through the power of Christ, bringing about miraculous healings to such an extent that people "carried out the sick into the streets, and laid them on beds and pallets, that as Peter came by at least his shadow might fall on some of them" (Acts 3:1–10, 5:12–15, 9:33–43). But we soon find that Peter waffles between the Christians who believe that all converts need to be circumcised and those who believe that they do not (Gal 2). He waffles even though he initially took the side of those who believed that Gentile converts didn't need circumcision (Acts 10–11), and oversaw the decision at the so-called "Council at Jerusalem" where circumcision was deemed unnecessary for Gentile converts (Acts 15:1–21). St. Paul, a Jewish convert previously hot on persecuting Christians, confronted Peter "to his face" after Peter withdrew from eating with the Gentile converts at Antioch—an act of cowardice caused by Peter "fearing the circumcision party" (Gal 2:11–12).

This is not, as some scholars declare, a sign of a hopelessly divided Church, Hebrews vs. Hellenists, but a record of the actual, very human need for reform that was going on from the beginning, where fundamental disagreements within the Church are mended and failures of individual members, even the most prominent miracle-workers like Peter, are criticized and forgiven.

That's a very important lesson straight out of Scripture: there is no pristine early Church; this reforming Church *is* the early Church.

During this time, the constant need for reform, for sorting things out in the face of difficulties, occurs in regard to issues both little and big. In Romans, we hear St. Paul give the following advice about lesser disagreements:

> Now accept the one who is weak in faith, but not for the purpose of passing judgment on his opinions. One person has faith that he may eat all things, but he who is weak eats vegetables only. The one who eats is not to regard with contempt the one who does not eat, and the one who does not eat is not to judge the one who eats, for God has accepted him. Who are you to judge the servant of another? To his own master he stands or falls; and he will stand, for the Lord is able to make him stand (Rom 14:1-4).

But Paul faces greater disagreements, ones that threaten to break the Church up into rival factions based upon who founded or taught the respective communities of each. Witness his first letter to the Church at Corinth:

> Now I exhort you, brethren, by the name of our Lord Jesus Christ, that you all agree and that there be no

divisions among you, but that you be made complete in the same mind and in the same judgment. For I have been informed concerning you, my brethren, by Chloe's *people,* that there are quarrels among you. Now I mean this, that each one of you is saying, "I am of Paul," and "I of Apollos," and "I of Cephas," and "I of Christ." Has Christ been divided? Paul was not crucified for you, was he? Or were you baptized in the name of Paul? (I Cor 1:10–13)

So much for the notion that there was only smooth sailing aboard the barque of the early Church. If that weren't enough to show the roughness of some of the waters, we have in the same letter to the Corinthians, St. Paul noting in dismay, "It is actually reported that there is immorality among you, and immorality of such a kind as does not exist even among the Gentiles, that someone has his father's wife. You have become arrogant and have not mourned instead, so that the one who had done this deed would be removed from your midst" (I Cor 5:1-2).

Apparently, some of the flock thought salvation did not exclude sexual practices that did "not exist even among the Gentiles" (pagans who, to understate it, accepted quite a lot when it came to sexual misbehavior). Christians were called to a higher standard.

Do you not know that your bodies are members of Christ? Shall I then take away the members of Christ and make them members of a prostitute? May it never be! Or do you not know that the one who joins himself to a prostitute is one body with her? For He says, "The two shall become one flesh." But the one who joins himself to the Lord is one spirit with Him. Flee immorality. Every other sin that a man commits is outside the body, but the immoral man sins against his own body. Or do you not know that your body is a temple of the Holy Spirit who is in you, whom you have from God, and that you are not your own? For you have been bought with a price: therefore glorify God in your body (I Cor 6:15–20).

Nor did it take long for doctrinal matters to need clarification and reform, as St. Paul makes clear in his letter to the Galatians:

I am amazed that you are so quickly deserting Him who called you by the grace of Christ, for a different gospel; which is really not another; only there are some who are disturbing you and want to distort the gospel of Christ. But even if we, or an angel from heaven, should preach to you a gospel contrary to what we have preached to you, he is to be accursed! As we have said before, so I say again now, if any man is preaching to you a gospel contrary to what you received, he is to be accursed! (Gal 1:6–9)

And there were not only doctrinal controversies among the Ephesians, but also a lapse into mythological ruminations and other distractions that kept Christians from focusing on the essentials of the faith, as St. Paul makes clear in his letter to Timothy, his co-worker in Christ:

As I urged you upon my departure for Macedonia, remain on at Ephesus so that you may instruct certain men not to teach strange doctrines, nor to pay attention to myths and endless genealogies, which give rise to mere speculation rather than furthering the administration of God which is by faith. But the goal of our instruction is love from a pure heart and a good conscience and a sincere faith. For some men, straying from these things, have turned aside to fruitless discussion, wanting to be teachers of the Law, even though they do not understand either what they are saying or the matters about which they make confident assertions. (I Tim 1:3–7)

Christians were also not above the equivalent of pew-rents, in their worship, bringing the rich forward for the good seats, and letting the poor, the very ones whom Christ himself preferred, sit in the least desirable places. This time it is St. James who calls for a reform.

My brethren, do not hold your faith in our glorious Lord Jesus Christ with an attitude of personal favoritism. For if a man comes into your assembly with a gold ring and dressed in fine clothes, and there also comes in a poor man in dirty clothes, and you pay special attention to the one who is wearing the fine clothes, and say, "You sit here in a good place," and you say to the poor man, "You stand over there, or sit down by my footstool," have you not made distinctions among yourselves, and become judges with evil motives? Listen, my beloved brethren: did not God choose the poor of this world to be rich in faith and heirs of the kingdom which He promised to those who love Him? But you have dishonored the poor man. Is it not the rich who oppress you and personally drag you into court? Do they not blaspheme the fair name by which you have been called? (James 2:1–7)

I don't think I need to multiply examples, which could be easily done, all showing that the New Testament itself clearly recounts the need, from the very beginning, for continual reform of all kinds among the faithful. We would be doing violence to the Bible to think that the earliest believers in the Church were somehow exempt from the difficulties, controversies, confusions, and all-too-human foibles that can be found among Christians at any time, when the revealed texts themselves reveal otherwise.

The *Didache*, the Earliest Catechetical Manual

We also have witness from one of the earliest, if not the earliest, extra-testamental document of the first Christians, the *Didache*, or as it's rendered into English, *The Teaching of the Twelve Apostles.*

The *Didache* is an amazing document, one that was used as a kind of short-form catechetical manual in the first century for converts coming into the Church from the pagan world. In it, we find instructions for the new faithful, telling them the immoral practices they must now give up, admonishing them to show a new charity even to their enemies, and giving converts the basics of doctrine, worship, and Church life.

But we also find very practical advice which shows us that it didn't take long for heretics, charlatans, and false prophets trying to make a profit to appear on the Christian scene. Concerning teachers, the *Didache* instructs believers to receive them, "But if the teacher himself turns and teaches another doctrine to the destruction of this, hear him not."[1] Likewise, an apostle or prophet should be welcomed, as long as he only stays one or two days, but "if he remains three days, he is a false prophet." The text adds that he should "take nothing but bread" and that if "he asks for money, he is a false prophet." It continues, "every prophet who teaches the truth, but does not do what he teaches, is a false prophet.... But whoever says in the Spirit, Give me money, or something else, you shall not listen to him."[2]

There were lay Christians who were also abusing the commanded charitable hospitality and becoming Christ-mongering moochers, so the *Didache* warns,

> But receive everyone who comes in the name of the Lord.... If he who comes is a wayfarer, assist him as far as you are able; but he shall not remain with you more than two or three days, if need be. But if he wants to stay with you, and is an artisan, let him work and eat. But if he has no trade, according to your understanding, see to it that, as a Christian, he shall not live with you idle. But if he wills not to do, he is a Christ-monger. Watch that you keep away from such.[3]

Belief in Need of Reform:
A String of Gnostic Heresies

All of the above occurred within the Church's first century. By the second century (or perhaps even a little earlier), heretical branches of Christianity were already sprouting off the main trunk. We'll look at one such heresy, Gnosticism.

There is a perennial temptation to look at all the evils of the world and the afflictions and passions of the body, and declare that the world and the body are evil, in fact so evil that the whole material world must have been created by an evil god, whereas the spiritual world was created by a good god. In the second century, that temptation flowered into the heresy of Gnosticism, which relied on those passages from the Gospels and St. Paul that contrasted the spirit with the evils of the flesh.

For example, in the Gospel of John, Jesus declares "Truly, truly, I say to you, unless one is born of water and the Spirit he cannot enter into the kingdom of God. That which is born of the flesh is flesh, and that which is born of the Spirit is spirit" (Jn 3:5–6). Then there is Paul's letter to the Galatians: "For the flesh desires what is contrary to the Spirit, and the Spirit what is contrary to the flesh. They are in conflict with each other, so that you are not to do whatever you want" (Gal 5:17). These were favorite Gnostic passages, picked out of orthodox Scripture. The Gnostic deviation spread alongside orthodox Christianity, and reappeared in multiple variations for centuries thereafter, oftentimes becoming the dominant form of Christianity in entire geographical regions.

The Gnostic Marcion of Sinope is worth looking at more closely. Marcion, who died in about AD 160, was originally a shipmaster, who must have done well, since he donated a huge amount of money to the Church in Rome. The Church gave it back because Marcion insisted on teaching (based on his reading of Scripture) that there was a good god and an evil god, a god of the spirit and a god of the flesh. The good god was Jesus' father, the purely spiritual god of the New Testament; the evil god was the god of the Old Testament, the material god who created the evil material world. He therefore declared that only a few writings of what we now consider to be the

New Testament were authentic (parts of the Gospel of Luke and large selections from the letters of St. Paul), but the entire Old Testament was to be thrown out. Salvation meant the spiritual escape from our bodies and the material world.

In fact, it was Marcion's attempt to define which of the Christian writings circulating in the second century were authentic that pushed the orthodox Christians to begin the process of *officially* declaring which writings were indeed divinely inspired. Against Marcion, the Church reaffirmed the entire Old Testament and what we now find in the New as Holy Scripture. The New Testament itself, we might say, is the result of reform, the early Church's formation of the biblical canon against a Christian heretic's attempt to deform it.

The Church's efforts did not make variations on Gnosticism disappear. An obvious implication drawn from Gnosticism and Marcionism was that, since Jesus was God, he could not really have become incarnate, let alone physically suffer on the cross and die, since the good spiritual god would have nothing to do with the evils of the world and the flesh. Therefore, Jesus just *appeared* to be in the flesh. The spin-off heresy from this belief was therefore called Docetism, from the Greek *dokein*, "to appear or seem." The Docetists bubbled up in the latter second century.

In the third century, a Persian prophet Mani interpreted the Scriptures along similar lines, arguing that there are two rival gods overseeing two rival worlds, the world of spirit and the world of matter. The heresy of Manichaeism likewise spread all over the Eastern Mediterranean, and flourished for several centuries thereafter.

Another offshoot of Gnosticism, this one thriving in Armenia between the seventh and ninth centuries, was the Paulician heresy, named after Paul of Samosata, a third-century bishop of Antioch. The proximate source of the heresy was an Armenian named Constantine or Constantine-Silvanus who lived near Samosata. Constantine was an avid reader of the New Testament, which inspired him to found a new congregation intent on *restoring* Christianity to its pure origins in St. Paul, as Constantine understood him—and he understood him as a Gnostic dualist, believing in an evil god of matter and a good god of spirit. As with Marcion, he rejected the Old Testament. Ironically, even heretics suffer the need for reform, the Paulicians soon breaking up into two rival sections, the Baanites (the traditionalists) and the Sergites (the reformers).

In the tenth century, we find the Bogomils, yet another variation of Gnosticism which appears to have arisen from the Paulicians in Bulgaria, and then spread all over Europe. They too thought that embracing a dualist interpretation of Christian Scripture was a return to the ancient pristine Church and rejected contemporary Church teachings and the Church hierarchy. They believed there were two sons of God, the elder Satanail and the younger Michael. The recalcitrant elder son was cast out for his rebellion and created the material world as an act of vengeance. The younger son reappeared in the form of Jesus.

Beginning in the 1100s and continuing for several centuries in southern France and northern Italy we find the Cathari, sometimes referred to as the Albigensians, who provide yet another form of spirit-flesh dualism. Given that the body was evil, the Cathari sought salvation through asceticism, which of course made them look much more holy than some of the rather worldly Catholic bishops, priests, and laypersons of the time, and they therefore won converts preaching and teaching among the Christian faithful. Given that matter and the body were evil, the Cathari rejected physical sacraments, including both baptism and the Eucharist. They were vegetarians, not because they were the first animal rights activists, but because anything born of sexual intercourse must be evil. Needless to say, that gave the Cathari an exceedingly dim view of marriage, since sex played into the devil's desire to entrap more spirits in fleshly bodies through procreation and draw humans to their doom through sexual pleasure itself.

We emphasize again that the Cathari took themselves to be a reform movement, one that was rooted in their reading of Scripture, and one that produced its own bishops and bishoprics in France and Italy. Thus, the whole line of these dualistic heresies we've just outlined came from (generally) sincere Christians who interpreted Scripture erroneously.

This is important for our understanding of the way the Catholic Church viewed Scripture and its reading by the laity. As a response to the spread of Catharism, one of the French bishops realized that the Church must do something, and therefore he called the Council of Toulouse (1229). Note the context: the widespread misreading of Scripture in the spirit of ancient Gnosticism was causing a heresy that brought believers to reject the body as evil, marriage as evil, the sacraments as evil, and even taking in food as evil. That is the context of the famous declaration made by the Council, "We prohibit also that the laity should be permitted to have the books of the Old and the New Testament; unless anyone from the motives of devotion should wish to have the Psalter or the Breviary for divine offices or the hours of the blessed Virgin; but we most strictly forbid their having any translation of these books."[4] A similar statement was repeated at the second Council at Tarragon (1234).

Drawing this section all together, we have shown that reform in regard to heresy was a part of Christianity's historical existence from

Paul's letters of apostolic correction to the larger, more organized heresies of the second century onward. We could have treated a host of other heresies to make the same point, such as the widespread heresies of Arianism or Pelagianism, the former of which denied the divinity of Christ, and the latter asserted that we could be saved by our own efforts without Christ.[5] (We'll discuss them later, in other contexts). But a focus on the persistent heresy of Gnosticism allows us to see very clearly one more reason why reform within the Church never ceases: in this illustrative case, the perennial temptation to deny the goodness of the body is just that, perennial, and it is an error that strikes at the orthodox heart of Christianity's affirmation of the goodness of all creation, the reality of the Incarnation, and the ultimate importance of the resurrection. It also shows us clearly that access to Scripture doesn't always translate into orthodoxy. Scriptural interpretation itself has been periodically in need of reform from the very beginning, and one very important reform resulted in the settling of what books are found in the New Testament.

Reforming Popes: The Tale of Two Gregories

We might have the notion, given some of the more virulent Protestant literature of the Reformation period (and thereafter), that there were simply no good popes, and the whole line was a wash of Antichrists whoring up and down Babylon. That view is as false as the Catholic literature that makes the line of popes stretching back to St. Peter one saint after another. There were, in fact, bad popes, and we'll meet them later. But in this chapter, since we're talking about the history of reformations, we'll meet two very good ones, Gregory I (540–604) and Gregory VII (1015–1085), two great reforming popes.

Gregory I, also known as Gregory the Great, is important (among other reasons) in that he is held to be a saint by Catholics, the Eastern Orthodox Church, and Anglicans, and esteemed by many Protestants. Gregory was a Roman noble by birth, but Rome itself was in steep decline. It had been sacked in 410 by the Germanic Visigoths led by King Alaric, in 455 by the Germanic Vandals under the leadership of King Genseric, and once again in 546 by the Germanic Ostrogoths under King Totila, during the devastating Gothic War of 535 to 554.

Another Germanic invasion occurred in the latter part of the 500s, this one by the Lombards, which didn't result in the sack of Rome, but in the filling of the city with a host of desperate refugees. We call these "barbarian invasions," and they certainly were barbaric, but we should add that these barbarians happened to be Christians who had been evangelized by Ulfilas (311–383) who taught the Germanic tribes the heretical Arian form of Christianity.

If such repeated assaults weren't enough to make Rome wretched, one of history's most horrible plagues—just as horrible as the later, more famous Black Plague of the fourteenth century— spread across the Empire from the east in 542, killing between twenty-five and fifty million people.

Such was the miserable condition of Rome when Gregory was "elevated" to its bishopric, "the first monk to become pope."[6] In one of his famous homilies on the Old Testament book of Ezekiel, Gregory broke out in lament, "cities have been destroyed, camps overturned, fields deserted, the earth emptied in solitude.... For since the Senate has failed, the people have perished, and the sufferings and groans of the few who remain are multiplied each day. Rome, now empty, is burning!"[7] The political order was crumbling, and Gregory had to step in not just as pope but as a kind of civic administrator.

He would rather have remained a humble monk, lamenting in a letter to the patriarch of Constantinople, who was also his old friend, "I have taken on an old and very broken down ship (for the waves pour in from all sides and the rotten planks, shaken by daily and powerful storms, suggest a shipwreck), [and so] I ask by our almighty Lord that in this danger of mine you stretch forth the hand of your prayer."[8]

In the midst of Rome's chaos, Pope Gregory (reigning from 590 to 604) led two great missionary efforts: one, to convert the Germanic Arians to the orthodox Catholic faith; and two, sending Augustine (not the earlier, more famous St. Augustine, but another) to the Anglo-Saxons to convert them from paganism (which is why the Anglican Church regards Gregory as a saint).

There was also, of course, need for reform in the Church itself, and Gregory was quick to admonish bishops who stole property, sought glory or temporal rewards rather than holiness, or sold Church offices for profit—a sin called simony.[9] Nor did Gregory spare the monastics, showing "no mercy if he learned of unlawful practices in monasteries," including disciplining a nun who sold goods from the convent so she could buy herself the post of prioress, a nun caught in fornication, monks living with nuns, and any monastics who otherwise broke their vows.[10] He fought against lay control of priests and bishops among the Franks, wherein a king would sell a bishopric to the highest bidder, "regardless of his spiritual qualifications"[11]—a problem that only got worse, despite Gregory's efforts at reform.

Gregory also reformed the liturgy, and gave us "Gregorian chant," but most striking of his achievements, at least from the standpoint of later charges against a rich, corrupt papacy, was his superhuman charity, emptying both his own and the Church's coffers to take care of the poor and destitute. The papacy had its own lands around Rome, and Gregory treated them as a primary source of charity for the needy.

In doing this, Gregory was following the mandate of the first Christians, clerical and lay. Christians who were well off understood that ultimately their wealth belonged to God, and God wished it to be used for the benefit of the poor. And so, Christians gave money and land.[12] Such was the reason why Gregory considered the possessions of the Roman Church in Italy, Sicily, Dalmatia, and Provence as (in his words) "the property of the poor."[13]

Nor did Gregory pull any papal punches with the wealthy to whom he preached, as one of his surviving homilies on Christ's parable of the rich man and Lazarus makes evident, where Gregory tells his hearers that the rich man "is rebuked not for having taken away the property of other people, but for not having given his own away."[14]

Such sermons likely inspired Rome's wealthy Christians who made great donations to the Church. Gregory immediately dispersed these resources wherever they were needed most and he was famous for not only dispatching monks to feed the hungry in Rome, but for inviting the poor to dine at his own table (and he chastised other bishops for not acting accordingly).[15]

Gregory's concern for the poor and the illiterate was highlighted in his defense of the Church's use of images and paintings to teach the gospel. In one famous letter, Gregory rebuked Serenus, bishop of Marseilles, for destroying paintings in his churches, presumably because Serenus felt they violated the biblical injunction against idolatry. Gregory reminded him of his central pastoral duty to preach to the poor. Painted images, Gregory reminds him, "have been made for the edification of ignorant people, so that, not knowing how to read, they might learn what was said by studying the actual story." Such pictures, Gregory said, were the Bible of the poor (especially, we might remember, in a time when there were no printing presses).[16]

It is difficult to find fault with such a man and such a pope, and if men like Gregory the Great had held the papacy in the half-century leading up to the Reformation, it's unlikely the Reformation would have occurred. Or if it had, it wouldn't have taken the shape it did, because the initial and urgent appeal of Luther was against the corruption of the papacy.

But reforms never cease, given the reality of sin. So we are not surprised to find that the papacy in the tenth century, the century before our next Pope Gregory, had indeed become corrupt. This string of really bad popes in the 900s has been called the Rule of the Harlots, or worse, the Pornocracy. These popes were not the only clerics who abused their positions. At the heart of the problem was lay control of Church appointments—in the case of the papacy in the tenth century, by a family from Tusculum, the Theophylacti.

The pattern of corruption of Church offices occurred, in great part, through original good intentions. From the time of the first Gregory onward, rich Christians who sincerely wanted to follow Christ's commands would use their money to build churches, monasteries, and even bishoprics on their land. This was all to the good, at first, because it was one of the primary ways in which actual churches and dioceses spread throughout Europe. Europe wouldn't have been Christianized by the time of the Reformation in the sixteenth century without these benefactions.

But soon the wealthy landowners began to consider these churches and monasteries to be part of *their* estate, and the revenues to be gathered from tithes to be *their* personal revenue. And what better place to put one's ne'er-do-well sons than in one of these "livings," as priest, abbot, or bishop? One doesn't need much experience in fallen humanity to realize that these sons would often be quite unworthy, quite unholy, and quite capable of milking the ecclesiastical holdings for all they were worth, all the while living a life of luxury and debauchery, fleecing whatever flock they'd been given.

This phenomenon is called, historically, by the more technical title "lay investiture," a tag that refers to the lay control of Church offices. The source of this corruption, again, is the notion that the landlord—a duke, prince, or king—controls Church holdings on his estate. Laymen also found that they could sell churches and monasteries to the highest bidder, if so inclined by whim, avarice, or necessity.

An offshoot of lay investiture was the less elegant form of piracy, the political commandeering by powerful noble families of lucrative Church offices through force and intrigue, making them a kind of family inheritance, such as was carried on by the above-noted Theophylacti family who hijacked the papacy in the tenth century and filled the chair of Peter with some of the most unworthy men to sit in a chair of any kind.

How to reform the Church if the pope himself is of the lowest moral caliber? The providential answer began during the Rule of the Harlots, not in Rome, but in the abbey of Cluny, founded in 910 by William I, duke of Aquitaine, also known as William the Pious. One of his most pious acts was to mandate that the abbey at Cluny could not be under lay control, nor could any bishop or even the pope interfere with it (a good move, given that the papacy was in the hands of the first of the bad popes, Pope Sergius III). The Cluniac Reform movement began as a reform of the Benedictine Order of monastics, but it became a great seed bed for a string of holy reforming popes, bishops, priests, and monks. One of its finest flowers was Pope Gregory VII (reigning from 1073 to 1085), who passionately sought to end the selling of Church offices, their inheritance within a family, and the state's efforts to control the Church through ecclesiastical appointments. As part of that reform, Gregory made clerical celibacy (a long-standing discipline of the Church that was being followed more in the breach than in the observance) mandatory and insisted that priests and bishops be wholly focused on their duties to the faithful and not with feathering familial nests financially or with appointments for profligate sons.

Ironically, the reform of the papacy was possible because the German King Henry III (who would become the Holy Roman Emperor) took it upon himself to end the string of bad popes (the last being the regrettable, twice-deposed and twice-restored Italian, Benedict X) by installing the German pope Damasus II (1048) who died within weeks of his elevation, and his successor, another German, Pope Leo IX, the first of the great reforming popes and a canonized saint. King Henry III was known as Henry the Pious and he considered Italy part of his estate and the purification of the Church in Rome as part of his Christian duty, which later proved, to all who knew their history, that reform of the Church was not solely a result of ecclesiastics but of a German king—something that should be kept in mind when we come to the Reformation five hundred years later.

Franciscans, Dominicans, and the Imitation of Christ

The necessity of monastic reform—or calls for abolishing the monasteries—was a major controversy of the Reformation.[17] But monastic reform was nothing new—and the Cluniac Reform movement was hardly alone. There was, for example, the great reform initiated by St. Francis of Assisi (1181–1226). Francis's Order of Friars Minor (the official name of the Franciscans) was designed to bring about reform within the structure of the Catholic Church, under obedience to the pope, by a joyful embrace of poverty, self-denial, and even personal humiliation and physical suffering.

St. Francis offered an orthodox alternative to the Waldensians, a similar back-to-apostolic-poverty reform movement allegedly begun by Peter Waldo (1140–1205). Waldo was a rich cloth merchant who, after radical conversion to the ideal of apostolic poverty, gave all he had to the poor, and took up a life of preaching. This was lay, Scripture-based preaching (from Scripture translated into the Romance vernacular), which he felt called to do as a statement against the failures of the materially comfortable Church hierarchy he renounced as unworthy of meriting obedience.

The Waldensians were originally papal approved for their adherence to apostolic poverty (1179), but, not long after St. Francis' birth, were condemned for their disobedience to the Church hierarchy (1184). Waldo died about the time that St. Francis had his famous spiritual conversion from a profligate son of a rich cloth merchant to a beggar for Christ. St. Francis would dress in rags, live with lepers, and preach the gospel wherever he went, and he also bore the painful stigmata on his hands, feet, and side.

While Francis was loyal to the pope, one might see in the Waldensians—who rejected the Church hierarchy as corrupt—a prefiguring of Reformation Protestantism, but there were important differences. Neither Luther nor Calvin nor any other major Protestant leader of the Reformation embraced apostolic poverty. The Waldensians styled themselves as a religious order, the Order of the Poor, and took vows of poverty, chastity, and obedience, which would put them at odds with Luther's doctrine of justification by faith and not works (works such as embracing poverty) and his rejection of religious orders and vows.

Another reform movement was the Order of Preachers (more popularly known as the Dominicans), founded by the Spaniard Dominic de Guzmán in 1215. The Dominicans preached the gospel of Catholic Christianity, especially against the Cathars, and embraced the poverty of Christ, begging for their food.

Another powerful reform movement was the fourteenth-century Modern Devotion, *Devotio Moderna*, a movement of clergy and lay men and women who embraced simplicity and piety, prayer and good works, and whose teaching inspired the immensely influential spiritual classic, allegedly written by Thomas à Kempis, *The Imitation of Christ*.

And Some Last-Minute Reformers

Nearly all reformers in the latter part of the 1400s and early 1500s were last-minute reformers, because they believed the world was about to end. Martin Luther certainly understood his actions as taken in the light of a looming apocalypse, and that accounts for his urgency.

But there was another famous and fiery monk whose tirades against corruption in Rome were, if anything, even more incendiary than those of the Augustinian friar Martin Luther in 1517. That monk would be the Dominican Girolamo Savonarola

(1452–1498). About Savonarola, it's been said that had he been listened to by the Church hierarchy, "perhaps beyond the Alps Luther would not have arisen, or his influence would have been less; and Reform, of which every Christian heart felt the need, would then have been born in the very bosom of the Church of Rome."[18]

By quoting these words, we are not making any judgment on Luther's doctrines, but noting the obvious fact that a holy scourging and scouring of Rome, as Savonarola believed God demanded, would have made the Holy See *the* source of Church-wide reform, rather than *the* obstacle to it, and such reform would have been working for some two decades before Luther's momentous challenge.

Savonarola was an exceedingly popular preacher, except, of course, with the papacy. The following comes from one of his most renowned sermons, which circulated as a pamphlet as well, "On the Renovation of the Church," given in Florence on January 13, 1495, when young Martin Luther was about twelve years old.

Because of its sins, Savonarola proclaimed, "all of Italy must be turned upside down, Rome as well, and then the Church must be renewed." Know that God is about to inflict grave punishments, when there is "at the head of government ambition, lust and other vices," and when you also see "that God permits the heads of the Church to be weighed down by evils and simonies," and furthermore, when you see among people in general, and Florence in particular, that "sinners are stubborn and do not want to turn to God and do not value or appreciate those who call them to lead good lives, but always proceed from bad to worse and are obstinate in their vices. . . ." He didn't let his fellow mendicant friars off the hook either, crying out, "O tonsured ones, tonsured ones! You are the cause of all this evil!"[19]

The whole Church was rotten and in need of the deepest reform, he said. Using a poignant scriptural metaphor about the barren fig tree (Mark 11:12–25), Savonarola declared that

> This fig-tree is the tree of the Church, which, though in the beginning it bore an abundance of fruit and no leaves, nevertheless is at the point today where it bears no fruit at all, but only leaves, that is, ceremonies and shows and superfluities whereby it overshadows the other plants of the earth—which means that the prelates of the Church because of their bad example are responsible for other men falling into very many sins. The gardener will come, that is, Christ, and will cut down this fig-tree which is fruitless. Therefore, the Church will renew itself.[20]

Savonarola declared that he had seen a vision of "a black cross above the Babylon that is Rome, upon which was written: *Ira Domini*," the Wrath of the Lord, and another vision of a "sword poised over Italy."

He continued, "if you are Christian, you have to believe that the Church must be renewed...so that men become good and go there [to Jerusalem] and convert the infidels [Muslims] to Christianity."[21] Many saw Islam—its conquest of the Holy Land and its constant threats against Europe—as a punishment for the sad state of the Church.

But the pope at the time, the notoriously corrupt Alexander VI, did not heed the call for reform. Instead, he excommunicated Savonarola in 1497. Savonarola was hanged in May 1498, and his body burned to keep devotees from collecting relics. The Catholic Church did call a reforming council just before Luther's challenge in 1517. The Fifth Lateran Council (1512–1517) is famous both for doing nothing and for the scorching opening statement by the reform-minded General of the Augustinian Order, Giles (or Egidio) Antonini, bishop of Viterbo, Italy.

Like Savonarola, Giles believed the Church's punishment for not reforming was imminent, and he congratulated the Council for finally taking up the task. This was hopeful thinking on his part, given that the pope in attendance was Pope Julius II who was (in the words of historian Eamon Duffy) "a very dubious Father of all the Faithful, for he had fathered three daughters of his own while a cardinal, and he was a ferocious and enthusiastic warrior, dressing in silver papal armour and leading his own troops through the breaches blown in city walls of towns who resisted his authority."[22]

Giles informed the Council that it had a duty "to root out vice, to arouse virtue, to catch the foxes who in this season swarm to destroy the holy vineyard, and finally to call fallen religion back to its old purity, its original splendor, and its own sources."[23] One suspects that Giles thought some of the foxes were among the shepherds assembled.

Much against the temper of Pope Julius, Giles declared that the only hope of the Church lay in councils, the implication being that it wasn't going to happen through this pope. But giving Julius the respectful benefit of the doubt, Giles informed the pope that God "commands you to tear down, root up, and destroy errors, luxury, and vice, and to build, establish, and plant moderation, virtue, and holiness." The Church conquers the world, not through arms (a bit of a sting for the "warrior pope," especially given that the papal armies had just been trounced by the French at the Battle of Ravenna), but by holiness. Giles then offered a lesson in Church history:

In the beginning relying on its own [spiritual] arms the Church gained Africa, took possession of Europe, occupied Asia. Not by war, not by the sword, but by the deeds of religion and the reputation of sanctity the Church carried the Christian banners throughout the entire world. But when the Bride [of Christ, the Church]...in her golden robes, exchanged the golden cloak of the burning spirit for the iron weapons of a mad Ajax, she lost the power born of the blood of the twelve Apostles, she abandoned Asia and Jerusalem, she was forced to relinquish Africa and Egypt, and she saw a good part of Europe together with the Byzantine Empire and Greece taken from her [by the Muslims].... So we see that when religion exchanges offerings for the sword in virtually the whole world the Church is struck, cast forth, and rejected to the immense profit of Mohammed, who, unless the sword is put down and we return again into the bosom of piety at the altars and shrines of God, will grow stronger day by day, will subjugate all to his power, and as the wicked avenger of our impiety will take possession of the entire world.[24]

The expansion of the Church was due to holiness, argued Giles, but then, having conquered the world, the Church became worldly, defending its very earthly possessions with the sword. The punishment, sent by God, was Islam, which took from Christendom by the sword what Christianity had originally gained through the Spirit. Unless the Council undergoes deep moral reform, "unless we force our greedy desire for human things, the source of all evils, to yield to the love of divine things, it is all over with Christendom, all over with religion...."[25] The need for reform was a crying need, crying to high heaven.

> When has our life been more effeminate? When has ambition been more unrestrained, greed more burning? When has the license to sin been more shameless? When has temerity in speaking, in arguing, in writing against piety been more common or more unafraid? When has there been among the people not only a greater neglect but a greater contempt for the sacred, for the sacraments, for the keys [of penance, given to Peter in Mt 16:18–19], and for the holy commandments? When has our religion and faith been more open to derision even of the lowest classes?[26]

It's a safe wager that the answer to these very pointed rhetorical questions was something along the lines of "never." One imagines, immediately after these words, that it was quiet enough to hear a *spillo* drop on the Lateran Basilica's floor. Then came some polite throat clearing, punctuated by a lot of side-glancing at Julius, before those present could get down to the difficult business of not doing anything while appearing to be busy.

In Sum...

It's clear from our history of Christianity up until the time of Luther that there never was a golden age of the Church when it was not in need of reform, and many within the Catholic Church were protesting in the early 1500s against the abuses of the clerical hierarchy, not just future Protestants. As we'll soon see, the earliest Protestants themselves immediately split with each other over how to reform, and, as I mentioned above, the history of Protestantism since the Reformation has been one of continual denominational splitting in the service of reform. Apostolic, Catholic, Eastern Orthodox, or Protestant—all are marked by controversy and division, corruption and renewal. The Church has always been, and will always be, in need of reform. Luckily for us, by God's grace, there have always been holy reformers ready to do the work, and so we dare hope, always will be until the end of time. But this brings us back to the central question of this book: what made the reform of 1517 into the Reformation? We'll begin by looking at something that made Martin Luther so angry that he believed reform of the Catholic Church was impossible.

CHAPTER THREE

Why the Papal States Were a Major Cause of the Reformation

R ather than throwing ourselves straightaway into an account of Martin Luther, we're first going to look more deeply and broadly into the causes of what made him and others so desperate and angry that they would turn a reformation into a Reformation, beginning with the most glaring: papal corruption. In the next chapter, we'll take a close and unpleasant look at corrupt popes themselves. Here, we'll focus on one of the chief causes, the great landholdings of the papacy, as justified by the fraudulent "Donation of Constantine."

Being a great landholder brought two kinds of corruption into the Catholic Church. First, it made the pope simultaneously a bishop who asserted universal spiritual authority and a king with very particular political and territorial aims as the ruler of the Papal States. Second, the political power and endowments of the Papal States tempted the unholy and unscrupulous to maneuver themselves onto the papal throne.

The pope as a great landholder is a bit difficult for us to imagine today since Vatican City now has the honor of being the smallest self-governing state in the world, about 110 acres, a little more than half the size of the average eighteen-hole golf course. Fascist dictator Benito Mussolini granted the Vatican this allotment as a way to resolve "the Roman Question" (what to do with the papacy in a united Italy) in the Lateran Accords of 1929. The accords had the unintended but beneficial effect of liberating the papacy from the burden and curse of its longstanding role of secular ruler; and if such an accord had been reached half a millennium before, there might have been no Reformation because many of the causes of Church corruption would have been removed.

Donations to the Roman Church (Including Constantine's and Pope Gregory's)

The roots of the Papal States go back to the Bible and the Book of Acts, where it is clear that the earliest of Christians understood that it was a good thing to give money or property or both to support the common life and evangelizing efforts of the infant Church (Acts 2:43–47; 5:1–4). As the Church grew, it attracted rich converts who donated their estates to the Church's service. These estates were often deeded to deacons or bishops, because under the laws of the pagan Roman Empire the Church itself could not own property, and such property if held "under the radar" was often at risk of being snatched during pagan persecutions.

Constantine was the first Roman emperor to become a Christian (in 312). After his conversion and the legalization of Christianity, the state allowed the Church to own property and Constantine ordered the restitution to the Church of lands lost during pagan persecutions.[1] For example, in a letter to Anullinus, the proconsul of Africa, he states: "We ordain that when this decree arrives, if anything which belonged to the Catholic Church of the Christians in a town or other place is still retained by citizens or others, you are to have it restored to the said churches immediately."[2]

On top of these imperial gifts, Constantine himself gave the bishop of the Church in Rome a "palace." During a stay in Rome, as historian Charles Odahl relates, the newly converted Constantine met Pope Miltiades. "The emperor reasoned that such an important Christian leader should have a residence appropriate to his status, and ceded the Lateran Palace from imperial estates at the eastern edge of the city to the Roman See."[3] The Lateran Palace was a great Roman home that originally belonged to a pagan noble family, the Laterani.[4]

Constantine also gave bishops money for their dioceses, exempted them from having to make financial contributions for public festivals, and built lavish churches, including the basilica next to the Lateran palace, which serves as the pope's cathedral and is now known as the Basilica of St. John Lateran.[5]

These were the original estates of the Roman Church, or the Papal Estates, and they were indeed gifts of Constantine, *dona* in Latin, from which we derive our English word, donation. Hence, considering it all in sum, there was, in fact, a donation of Constantine, a historical reality underneath the later, much-maligned, semi-fictional document, the "Donation of Constantine."

Constantine wasn't the only one giving gifts to the Church of Rome. For several centuries, rich lay members augmented the papal estates with further gifts of land. Pope Gregory the Great (590–604) himself was from a wealthy Roman family with estates around Rome and in Sicily. These he considered the Church's property, with their resources to be used for the benefit of the poor. It's accurate to call these estates the Donation of Gregory; and there were more donations to come—the most important from a Frankish king.

The Donation of Pepin

From the sixth century through the eighth century, Rome was menaced by the Lombards whose continual invasions of northern Italy drove waves of refugees into Rome, threatened the estates surrounding Rome (and hence Rome's food supply), and severed Rome's link to the Byzantine Empire (itself not an entirely friendly power) by seizing the Byzantine outpost of Ravenna, about 175 miles north of Rome, in 751. With Ravenna lost, Pope Stephen II turned to the Franks for help against the Lombards. He crossed the Alps to the court of King Pepin the Short (the father of Charlemagne) who promised he would regain lands seized by the Lombards and give them back to the papacy. In a treaty concluded at Pavia (the court of the Lombard king), the Lombards were compelled to "make the restitutions to the Pope through the agency of deputies of the Frankish King." Historian Eugen Ewig writes, "Thus did the 'Papal States' become a reality"[6] (or a larger reality) through the donation of Pepin.

"The creation of the Papal States, the so-called patrimony of St. Peter, made the pope a feudal lord, giving a real financial value to his office. The Chair of St. Peter became a prize for the great families of Rome and its neighborhood," adds historian E. R.

Chamberlin, "creating a more insidious danger for the Papacy than that which Byzantines and Lombards had threatened."[7]

At the time, the union of pope and king in the Papal States (or "The republic of St. Peter,"[8]) was an act of restoration that allowed the pope to better provide for his flock and that helped guarantee his independence from the Byzantine Empire, some of whose religious and political leaders thought that the pope should be made subordinate to Constantinople. So while the Papal States were a source of trouble in the future, at the time they seemed a great reestablishment of civilized order to turbulent portions of Italy.

The "Donation of Constantine"

Now we come to the great fraud—though it took centuries to be exposed as such: the document known as the "Donation of Constantine." An obvious double question about the "Donation of Constantine," once it's recognized that it wasn't written by the actual Constantine, is who wrote it and when. The scholarly answers are something like, "We don't know," and "Sometime during the period stretching from the pontificates of Pope Stephen II (752–757) and Adrian I (772–795)."[9]

In any event, "The most famous forgery was...without practical, political, juridical significance at the time of its composition," concludes Thomas Noble, because it was never used to justify anything in the eighth century. Yet, "the document was written in the Lateran during the early years of the...[Republic of St. Peter's] existence and it may be read as an indicator of certain attitudes in that crucial place, at that crucial time."[10]

What exactly is it? The document "Donation of Constantine" purports to be, among other things, an authentic deeding of even greater grants of land to Pope Sylvester (bishop of Rome, 314–335) from the recently converted Constantine. For five hundred years now, we've known the document is a fraud, and not an innocent one, because in the centuries that followed its composition, the "Donation of Constantine" became a rationale for the papacy to claim ever-greater temporal power and hence become ever more worldly.

The "Donation" was famously and decisively debunked around the year 1440 by Lorenzo Valla, an Italian humanist and Catholic priest, who wrote a withering analysis of the "Donation," *De Falso Credita et Ementita Constantini Donatione Declamatio*. Lorenzo's exposition was championed by the German nationalist and despiser of all things Italian, Ulrich von Hutten, who provided the first printed edition in 1517, a year that should ring a bell. Hutten was, not coincidentally, a passionate supporter of Martin Luther. When Luther discovered the "Donation of Constantine" was a fake, he spewed some of the most violent anti-papal rhetoric on this side of Voltaire, and his break with Rome became inevitable.

Taking a clear-eyed look at the document, we find the "Donation" freely mixes fact with fiction, and piety with exaggerated claims for papal political power.[11] Besides being a fraud, the greatest problem caused by the "Donation" was *not* that it was used by later popes to lord it over emperors. This was *a* problem, but most emperors, it turned out, could stand a bit of lording over from someone. No, the greatest problem was that its grand claims helped make the papacy, and its lands, a target for unscrupulous adventurers like the Borgias and the Medicis who viewed the papal office as a way to enrich themselves by treating the Church as a piously veiled familial syndicate for fleecing the sheep. The greatest source of corruption in the Catholic Church had nothing to do with religion *per se*; it was the worldly power claimed by the Church and justified by the fraud of the "Donation of Constantine."

A Papal "I Told You So" in Advance

Learning from experience is always more costly and destructive than learning before experience. In the last part of the 400s, Pope Gelasius warned of twin dangers: emperors who assumed the powers of a pope, and popes who assumed the powers of emperors.

Political and ecclesiastical powers must be kept separate, declared Gelasius. If they are united in one man who is a king, he will use the Church for his own political gains. If they are united in one man who is a pope, the pope will become just another king protecting his lands using the powers of the Church. Jesus Christ himself demanded the two powers be kept separate, and Gelasius asserts that after Christ, who was both king and priest, any union of king and priest is of the devil. In Gelasius's eloquent words, king and priest, emperor and pope, have two distinct functions that must not be confused:

> For Christ, mindful of human frailty, regulated with an excellent disposition what pertained to the salvation of his people. Thus he distinguished between the offices of both powers [of the state and the church, king and priest] according to their own proper activities and separate dignities, wanting his people to be saved by healthful humility and not carried away again by human pride, so that Christian emperors would need priests for attaining eternal life and priests would avail themselves of imperial

regulations in the conduct of temporal affairs. In this fashion spiritual activity would be set apart from worldly encroachments and the "soldier of God" (2 Timothy 2:4) would not be involved in secular affairs, while on the other hand he who was involved in secular affairs would not seem to preside over divine matters. Thus the humility of each order would be preserved, neither being exalted by the subservience of the other, and each profession would be especially fitted for its appropriate functions.[12]

Even if Constantine had really given to Pope Sylvester everything in the forged "Donation of Constantine," the pope should have given it right back, Gelasius would have advised. For otherwise the papacy would be debased by "worldly encroachments" and the pope "involved in secular affairs," which is, in fact what happened with the pope as ruler of the Papal States, however innocent and justified the beginning of it all may have been.

We surmise, then, that Pope Gelasius would have smiled with relief when, in 1929, the Papal States were forcibly shrunk to about the size of the original, historical donation of the actual Constantine, and even more when Pope Paul VI, the last pope crowned with the papal tiara, a sign of his temporal power, laid that tiara down, once and for all, on the altar of St. Peter's Basilica, and donated the equivalent of its worth to the poor—an act that would surprise Luther, and another sign that the Reformation was ending.

CHAPTER FOUR

The "Bad Popes" Really Were Bad

For Luther, and many others who became Protestants of one kind or another, the papacy was irredeemably bad, an assessment based upon the sad state of the popes at the time, one that led to the "whore of Babylon" epithet slung at the papacy as a whole. As a reaction, Catholics sometimes overlook or underplay the reality of bad popes, or even pretend there's been nothing but saints in the chair of St. Peter since Peter himself sat in it. For the sake of a much clearer understanding of the Reformation and of the papacy itself, we need to get to the actual truth.

The Catholic Church itself takes a more measured approach and hence is admirably parsimonious in recognizing popes as saints historically, even if the Church has had a good run lately. Three twentieth-century popes have been canonized—St. Pius X (1903–1914), St. John XXIII (1958–1963), and St. John Paul II (1978–2005)—and two are on the way: Venerable Pius XII (1939–1958) and Blessed Paul VI (1963–1978).

The vast majority of popes, about 70 percent, have not been declared saints. If canonization were a propaganda program by the Church, then it would have handed out "St." status to one pope after another. But what we actually find is good periods of papal history, and bad. There is a flood of saint-popes from St. Peter up through the beginning of the sixth century, and then a tapering off over the next two-plus centuries. In the period from Pope Stephen VI (896–897) to Benedict IX (1047–1048), and from Gregory XI (1370–1378) to Clement X (1670–1676) there were two big dry spells (with one notable exception, St. Pius V, 1566–1572).

While admitting that there certainly may have been quite saintly men in the papacy during the dry periods that the Church hasn't officially recognized, there are also a string of acknowledged bad popes too. As mentioned previously, the first dry/bad period was in the tenth century, and the acknowledged failures of that period led to the great reforms of St. Gregory VII (1073–1085). The second dry/bad period surrounded the Reformation, before, during, and somewhat after. And beyond the seventeenth century? There are no declared saints but only two "blessed" popes from Clement X in the late seventeenth century up to the end of the nineteenth century. It's not till we come to the twentieth century that we find, as with the first centuries of the Church, a string of saint-popes. Another sign, I believe, that the Reformation is coming to an end.

The Complex Causes of the Papal Dark Ages of the Tenth Century

One of the most pungent condemnations of the tenth century papacy came from a very pious Catholic cardinal, Cardinal Baronius, in his magisterial multi-volume *Ecclesiastical Annals*, a history undertaken at the request of a great Catholic reformer, St. Philip Neri (1515–1595). St. Philip Neri requested Cardinal Baronius to write his history as an antidote to a Protestant historical skewering of the Catholic Church written by Lutheran scholars at Magdeburg.[1] But he asked Cardinal Baronius for the truth, not counter-propaganda. It was the good cardinal who gave us the most instructive epithet for this period, the *saeculum obscurum*, the dark ages. For historians, the Dark Ages run from about AD 410 (the sacking of Rome) to AD 1000, and mark the breakdown of the political and economic structures of the western Roman Empire. For the Church, within that larger darkness, they run from 904 to at least 964 when the German Emperor Otto I began trying to reform the papacy.

In the century prior to the papal dark ages, there appeared to be a bit of light when Pope Leo III crowned Charlemagne as the first Holy Roman Emperor on Christmas Day, 800. The blessing of political order, which no Christian should ever foolishly underestimate, and the bright burst of learning and ecclesiastical flourishing of the Carolingian Renaissance did not, alas, last for long. Charlemagne's son, Louis the Pious (reigning 814–840) earned his moniker well enough, keeping the Empire together, but his surviving sons, Charles the Bald, Louis the German, and Lothar not only divided their inheritance but mismanaged it badly.

Thus began the political disintegration and subdivision that ended, by the tenth century, with lesser kings with baser instincts scrapping over smaller territories, the tragedy accompanied by ever more tenuous claims of these kings to be the next emperor. The resultant territorial shards were the pieces out of which modern Europe would be rebuilt some centuries later.

Advancing the cause of rack and ruin were invasions by Muslims, Magyars, and Vikings, with the Muslims making significant headway into Italy, even penetrating to the very walls of Rome in 843, where they pillaged both St. Peter's and St. Paul's basilicas.

"The result of all these fierce incursions, and of the intestine wars waged by kings and nobles for the name of emperor or for personal independence, for rivalry or for revenge," historian Horace Mann justly notes, "was, of course, widespread anarchy, ignorance, and immorality among all classes, both among the clergy and the laity."[2]

In short, the darkest age of the papacy was not a singular achievement of papal corruption in an otherwise morally sunny time, but a predictable and lamentable effect of a general, heavy darkness enveloping all of western Europe. Continues Mann, "Taking every advantage of the troubles which had come upon the fallen empire of the West, the nobles generally made themselves absolute masters in their own dominions, and did just as they thought fit."[3] One of the things they thought fit was stuffing family members into Church offices for profit.

The lay commandeering of churches and monasteries for riches and power was a problem throughout Europe. "The wealth of some of the larger monasteries and episcopal sees caused them to be much coveted by the powerful. Greedy nobles seized them by force or contrived to intrude into them some members of their own families."[4] Needless to say, since their motives were morally impaired, their candidates to become abbots and bishops were often rotten apples, rakes, and rounders, and Rome was not spared its share.

Papal Corruption and Reform in the Dark Ages

We've already mentioned the infamous Theophylacti family. The paterfamilias, Theophylact (circa 864–925), was a count from Tusculum who, with his wife Theodora, became Rome's ruler (circa 905) and made the papacy a familial appointment.

"Theodora was a shameless harlot," we are told by a contemporary chronicler, and her two daughters were, "not just her equals but if anything faster in the exercise of Venus."[5] Theodora's daughter Marozia herself ruled Rome as Senatrix between 926 and 932. Marozia was also the mistress of the notorious Pope Sergius III (904–911),[6] who was villain enough to have ordered the killing of his two immediate predecessors and to be the only pope to have his own illegitimate son put on the throne of St. Peter (the future John XI).

Among her mother Theodora's alleged lovers was Bishop John of Ravenna.[7] She brought him to Rome and enthroned him as Pope John X (914–928). She did so in part to increase her power, and in part (so we are assured) for her sexual convenience, "lest she should enjoy her lover by very rare beddings on account of the length of the two hundred miles that separate Ravenna from Rome...."[8] It seems likely that the machinations and political and ecclesiastical power of Theodora and Marozia gave birth to the myth of a female pope, Pope Joan (the female source of papal power remaking the name "John" in later retellings).[9]

Marozia hated her mother's alleged paramour Pope John X, and wanted her own son John on the papal throne instead, the result being that John X ended up in a dungeon, soon to be suf-focated by Marozia and her accomplices. "Once he was dead, they appointed John, the son of this same Marozia, as pope, whom that prostitute had conceived with Sergius."[10] Her son became pope at about the age of twenty, taking the name John XI (931–935). And the corruption was just getting started.

So we are told anyway. The only problem with this story is that nearly all of it comes from a single source, Bishop Liudprand of Cremona (920–972), whom our contemporary historians generally distrust, since he made significant factual confusions, and, as a man on the side of the Holy Roman Emperor in conflict with Rome, had a deeply vested interest in painting the Italians with a brackish brush.[11]

The Germanic Holy Roman Emperor at the time, Otto I, was bent on impressing his imperial rule over Italy. He had been crowned by another Theophylact pope, John XII (955–964). Otto, however, was also bent on reforming a corrupt papacy that wouldn't reform itself. He took the drastic solution of deposing Pope John XII, and putting his own candidate on the throne, Leo VIII.

But Pope John XII refused to back down, and a wrestling match between supporters of John and of Otto began, although Pope John (Liudprand assures the reader) soon died while he "was taking his pleasure with the wife of some man on a certain night outside of Rome." The cause of death: "he was struck in the temple by the devil so that within the space of eight days he had died of the wound" on February 26, 964.[12]

Whatever credence we give to Liudprand's scandalous account of the details, it is quite certain that the papacy was in great need of reform because it had been hijacked by ignoble local nobles.

Salvation finally came through another emperor, Henry III (1046–1056), who definitively ended the rogue rule of the Theophylacts and other corrupt Italian families by putting reform-minded Germans on the papal throne, leading to the epitome of reforming popes, St. Gregory VII (an Italian), the second reforming Gregory. Such are the general outlines of the dark age of the papacy, beginning with Pope Sergius III in 904 and ending either with Emperor Otto I's intervention in 964 (the traditional marker), or really with the last of the Theophylacts, the scandalous Pope Benedict IX, who was deposed in 1048.

The Avignon Papacy, Plagues, and Papal Schism

The next bad period for the papacy was its so-called "Babylonian Captivity" when the popes abandoned Rome for Avignon in southern France (1305–1377). This was the result of a long-standing dispute between the French King Philip IV and the Church. Philip wanted to raid church coffers in France to pay for his wars against England. Pope Boniface VIII (1294–1303) did not appreciate his bishops being kidnapped, robbed, or forbidden by the king to attend a papal council; and did not appreciate the king's whipping up anti-papal sentiment. In response, he issued his famous papal bull *Unam Sanctam* (1302), which declared that temporal power was entirely subordinate to papal power and that the French king had no right to make the French Church a royal appendage, a mere national Church:

> We are taught by the words of the Gospel that in this [one, universal, catholic] church and in her power there are two

swords, a spiritual one and a temporal one (Luke 22:38)....
Both...are in the power of the church, the material sword
and the spiritual. But the one is exercised for the church,
the other by the church, the one by the hand of the priest,
the other by the hand of kings and soldiers, though at the
will and sufferance of the priest. One sword ought to be
under the other and the temporal authority subject to the
spiritual power.[13]

Philip not surprisingly was unconvinced by *Unam Sanctam*,
and declared Pope Boniface a heretic and tried to have him kidnapped and brought to trial in France.

Having failed to kidnap the pope (who died after being beaten
by Philip's thug emissary), Philip decided to kidnap the papacy
itself, strong-arming the College of Cardinals into electing a
Frenchman, Clement V, who soon decided the city of Rome was
not for him and pulled up papal stakes for Avignon, arriving in
1309.

The College of Cardinals in Avignon was stacked with French-
men, who kept electing French popes who became ever more
worldly and beholden to the French monarchy. "Materialism
increased as the papacy became more deeply involved in politics,
in part due to Clement. He was clearly involved in simony as well
as nepotism, and he initiated a tax in which the first year of revenue
from the benefices sold went directly to the pope. As a result, the
papal treasury increased substantially."[14] In France, that is.

The low point of the Avignon papacy was, perhaps, Pope John
XXII (1316–1334). John was "also a Frenchman and an expert in
canon and civil law. In his seventies at his election, John survived

eighteen years, long enough to shape the Avignon papacy. Considered to be the 'Midas pope,' John dressed in gold cloth and slept on ermine fur, continuing to prosper even more through simony, the sale of indulgences, and the collection of taxes."[15]

Or perhaps the low point arrived with another Clement, Clement VI (1342–1352), who finished the building of the Avignon papal palace. "A great appreciator of luxury and wealth, Clement elevated papal materialism to its highest point. Ornate and lavish, the palace included banquet halls and gardens, a steam room for the pope, towers and courtyards, and chapels with frescoes and rose windows."[16]

The Avignon papacy, its French captivity, and its worldliness undermined papal prestige and authority, especially after the calamity of the Black Plague, one of the great scourges of history, which spread from the trade routes of the far east to southern and then northern Europe, killing up to two hundred million people. As historian Heather Para notes, "The plague decimated the population and left the tattered remnants of civilization in its wake, shaken and bewildered." The people naturally

> attributed their woes to divine retribution for sinful living. In looking for an explanation for their unbelievable ordeal, many pointed to the immoderation of the Avignon papacy. The excesses of the papacy, the absence of spiritual leadership, the opulent lifestyles of the papal court, the sinful behavior of bishops and popes, and the simony and sale of indulgences, all added up to what appeared to be the reason for the suffering and losses from the plague.[17]

To his credit, Pope Clement VI rolled up his silken episcopal sleeves when the plague hit Avignon hard in January 1348, and did his best to take care of the people of the city, as by the thousands corpses began piling up until about half the population was dead. Clement ended up fleeing the city himself in May. The plague was not finished, however, and hit Europe in wave upon wave, right up until the late 1600s. To the reformers in Luther's time, the connection between the plague and the lamentable state of the papacy was not something distant, but a present reminder of God's judgment on the corruption of the papacy.

The selling of indulgences, which Luther so hated, could also be traced back to Avignon. Pope Clement VI had declared 1350 a Jubilee Year and that penitential punishment of sins could be remitted for pilgrims to holy sites or by purchased indulgences that would fund the good work of the Church. This seemed a good investment to many, and the treasury of Avignon (and the number of pilgrims to Rome) rose accordingly. [18]

The Avignon papacy finally ended when St. Catherine of Siena convinced Pierre Roger de Beaufort, Pope Gregory XI (1370–1378) to return the papacy to Rome, which he did in January 1377.

After Gregory's death only a few months later, the Romans were in no mood for another French pope, and the timorous French cardinals consented to the election of the Italian Bartolomeo Prignano, who took the name, Urban VI.

Timorous they might have been, but as the disgruntled French cardinals retreated to Avignon, they split Christendom and humiliated the papacy even further by electing a Frenchman, who took the name Clement VII, as a rival pope. Thus began an embarrassing series of popes and antipopes, resulting in a schism that wasn't healed until the Council of Constance (1414–1418).

The Popes Leading Up to Luther

The Council of Constance settled on Martin V (1417–1431) as pope of the universal Church. He was an Italian, and a number of Italian-born popes followed, some of whom did try to reform the Church. In 1455, the cardinals elected an Italian-Spanish candidate, Alfonso Borgia, who took the name Callixtus III. Callixtus was actually a holy man, intent not only on cleaning up the papacy, but also in fighting off the incessant threat of Muslim invasion. He vowed never to rest until he recovered Constantinople, the great city of the Byzantine Empire that had fallen in 1453 to the Ottoman Turks.[19]

While Callixtus was a nearly blameless pope, he did commit one costly act of nepotism. He appointed his nephew Rodrigo de Borgia a cardinal, which became his stepping stone to the papacy. Rodrigo took the imperious name of Alexander VI (1492–1503), and was a pope so notoriously corrupt that he earned the praise of Machiavelli.

But corruption had already tainted the papacy by then. A predecessor of Alexander, Sixtus IV (1471–1484), marks the beginning of the so-called Renaissance popes, whose concerns were far more worldly than spiritual.

Sixtus IV won election through massive bribery of the cardinal electors and once firmly enthroned turned "the Papal State[s] into an Italian principality by recourse to all means, lawful and unlawful, and at the unseemly promoting of the Pope's relatives,"[20] endowing them with rich bishoprics and abbeys. One of the relatives, Giuliano della Rovere, his nephew, would later become Pope Julius II (1503–1513), "the Warrior Pope," during whose reign young Martin Luther would enter the Augustinian Order as a monk. Sixtus made five other nephews into cardinals as well.

The outcome of all this papal nepotism, as Eamon Duffy notes, "was the creation of a wealthy cardinalatial class, with strong dynastic connections"[21] and a papacy controlled by aristocratic Italian families, warring with each other as well as with other European monarchs.

The above-named notorious Borgia pope, Alexander VI, best illustrates the dire need for reform. "That such a man should have seemed a fit successor to Peter speaks volumes about the degradation of the papacy," laments Duffy.[22] Upon the death of Pope Innocent VIII (1484–1492)—who was apparently not that innocent, having fathered two children before becoming a priest, and rewarding them richly after becoming a pope—the conclave to elect a new pope convened in early August 1492. As historian Ludwig Pastor notes, a Spanish bishop, Bernardino Lopez de Carvajal, began by drawing "an impressive picture of the melancholy condition of the Church, and exhorted the Assembly to make a good choice and choose quickly."[23]

As was (sadly) usual for the time, papal elections were decided by bribery, involving both kings and nobles dropping huge sums from without, and rich cardinals buying their way onto the papal throne from within. Charles VIII of France reportedly put two hundred thousand ducats on his favorite, Giuliano della Rovere, who would become pope soon enough. But a dark horse, Rodrigo Borgia, quite rich himself, won through offering even more lavish bribes to the various cardinals in the form of ripe bishoprics, abbeys, towns, and other benefices with handsome yearly earnings, which quickly got him within one vote of victory.[24]

Opposition was adamant, but finally the ninety-six-year-old Cardinal Maffeo Gherardo was convinced to side with Borgia, who was then proclaimed Pope Alexander VI on the morning of

August 11, 1492 (eight days after Christopher Columbus set sail on his famous voyage). So it was that "a man attained to the highest dignity, who in the early days of the Church would not have been admitted to the lowest rank of the clergy, on account of his immoral life."[25]

In his notorious book, *The Prince*, Machiavelli remarked, "Alexander VI never did anything, nor ever thought of anything, but how to deceive men,"[26] adding that, "of all the pontiffs there have ever been he showed how far a pope could prevail with money and forces."[27] Not insignificant praise from a man whose forte was counseling rulers on the fine art of ruthless advancement.

Of all the renaissance popes, Alexander is perhaps the most infamous. Among his failings, he was a champion violator of his vow of clerical celibacy:

> Cardinal Borgia had more than a few illegitimate children, the mothers of the first three (Pedro Luis, Isabella, Girolama) being unknown. He then had four children with Vannozza dei Cattanei (one of his many mistresses). The four children—Giovanni (Juan), Cesare, Goffredo (Jofré), and Lucrezia—were born between 1474–1482, and were openly acknowledged by Cardinal Borgia who used his power when he became Pope Alexander VI to lavish gifts and honors upon all.... While pope, Alexander's passion soon fell upon Giulia Farnese, a beautiful woman already married to Orsino Orsini. She would move into a palace next to the Vatican (staying with the pope's illegitimate daughter, Lucrezia). She claimed a daughter, Laura, by the pope, and would remain his mistress until around 1500.[28]

While many of the scandalous rumors about Alexander's debauchery floating around Italy and Europe at the time were mongered by those who benefitted from exaggeration, as Eamon Duffy notes, "The sober truth about his sexual appetite and his single-minded devotion to his family, however, was scandalous enough." Devotion to his offspring turned Alexander's papacy into a political-dynastic struggle issuing from the Papal States outward, with Alexander often acting as a temporal prince in the Machiavellian sense, rather than as the prince of the Church. "As pope he systematically used his children's dynastic marriages to form alliances with a succession of princes. He also alienated large tracts of the papal lands to create independent duchies for his sons Juan and Cesare."[29] It was Cesare Borgia whom Machiavelli took as his model "prince," a man entirely devoid of the encumbrances of conscience.

Following Alexander's death in August 1503, there came Pius III, who was pope for less than a month before expiring, to be followed by Pope Julius II. Julius was a declared enemy of the Borgias. As Duffy notes, he was "the most ferocious pope of the period" and was "known to his contemporaries as *il terrible*, an untranslatable word that suggests a violent force of nature rather than a personality, Julius stormed up and down the Italian peninsula in his suit of silver armour at the head of his own troops."[30]

Somewhat to his credit, the warrior pope was not trying to add land to a family dynasty, but to liberate papal lands from secular control, especially those doled out by Alexander VI to his family.[31] But in his single-minded focus of regaining papal lands "there is no escaping the utterly secular character of such a pope. It was said of him that there was nothing of the priest about him but the cassock, and he did not always wear that."[32]

Martin Luther visited Rome in the winter of 1510–1511, during Julius II's pontificate, on behalf of his Augustinian Order, and was repulsed by the corruption he found. He spent his time in Rome, ironically, celebrating masses and undergoing personal penances to free his family members from purgatory.[33] Julius died in 1513, the same year Luther became a professor of biblical theology at the newly created University of Wittenberg. The next pope, the one who would be directly challenged by Luther and who eventually excommunicated him, was Pope Leo X (1513–1521), a member of the Medici family.

After Leo, we have the only Dutchman ever to hold the papal office, the saintly Adriaan Florensz (Pope Adrian VI, 1522–1523) who threw himself into reform, but enjoyed too short a pontificate to see any real fruit. After that, the cardinals returned to the Medici family, electing Clement VII (1523–1534) who is considered the last of the Renaissance popes. He was followed by Paul III (1534–1549) of the wealthy and powerful Farnese family. His beginnings were certainly those of a Renaissance pope—fathering five children with a mistress—but he surprised everyone, including perhaps himself, by initiating a true reformation within the Catholic Church, the so-called Counter-Reformation. Martin Luther died on February 18, 1546, during Paul III's pontificate, just as the Catholic Church was beginning its great reforming efforts with the Council of Trent (1545–1563) and trying to put behind it much of the corruption that had inflamed Luther's anger and inspired the Protestant revolt. But there is no denying the righteousness of that anger that gave rise to the revolt.

CHAPTER FiVE

Atheism and Paganism Played a Big Part in the Reformation

We may now shift our focus from inside to outside of the Church, to those who rejected Christianity completely—a largely ignored aspect of the Reformation. The usual story is that secular unbelief came *after* the Reformation and was the result of two things: religious wars caused by doctrinal disagreements that discredited Christianity's moral claims and the advent of modern science that discredited its cosmological foundations. But the truth is that aggressive atheism was taking hold in Europe long *before* the Reformation and that aggressive atheists *used* the Reformation to advance their cause.

In fact, the source of *modern* atheism is *ancient* atheism, which was rediscovered, along with the rediscovery of pagan philosophy, during the early Renaissance. Some Renaissance intellectuals believed that this ancient atheism was liberating, wise, and good; and they disparaged its historical and cultural displacement by moralistic, guilt-inducing Christian superstition. This preference for ancient atheism, which began among a few intellectuals in the century before Luther, claimed more and more adherents during the Reformation, and gained steam in the next centuries until it has become a dominant view in much of elite Western opinion. These secular liberal elites are now the very ones so successfully attacking Christianity for control of the culture, five hundred years after the Reformation.

Its pagan roots were recognized when it resurfaced in the Renaissance, and were often traced back to an ancient Greek materialist foe of religion, Epicurus (341–270 BC) and his Roman disciple Lucretius (99–55 BC). Indeed, atheists at the time of Luther were often called, among other epithets, "Epicureans."[1] The pagan influence was real, not imagined. Epicurus' and Lucretius' writings were rediscovered and circulated in the fifteenth century and became the foundation for modern philosophical materialism, which in turn provided the intellectual framework for modern scientific materialism that looked to banish God, the soul, miracles, and the afterlife, and hence Christianity, from the cosmos. The materialist Marxists, who come from this school, tried more directly to exterminate Christianity from the face of the earth.

Given the immense influence of Epicureanism, some idea of its central philosophical doctrines will help us understand its essential antagonism to Christianity. Epicurus was a materialist who claimed that there were only two things, ultimately, in the universe: eternal material atoms and the void or space between them.[2] Therefore, human beings had no immaterial souls,[3] and were not subject to punishments from the gods either in this life or in the afterlife.[4] Knowing we had nothing to fear from the gods allowed us— finally!—to be free of all the anxiety of facing divine judgment. Epicurus told his disciples that they should "Get used to believing that death is nothing to us," for death is merely the dissipation of our atoms; "when death is present, then we do not exist."[5]

Epicurus believed that he was saving humanity from its anxious fretting about Hades, and since Epicurus' time, Christianity had made Hades all the more vivid with its doctrine of hell. In order to understand the impact of the rediscovery of Epicurus in the 1400s, we only need to remind ourselves of how distressed Martin Luther was in the early 1500s worrying that his sinful inability to please God would lead to eternal torment in hell, a fear that he resolved with his pronouncement that we are saved by faith alone.

What the doctrine of *sola fide* did for Luther, the philosophy of Epicurus did for others. While Luther was relieved by the thought that he could be assured of heaven by the gift of faith, Epicureans were equally relieved by the thought that neither God nor hell existed. Over time, of course, Epicurus' answer has gained in popularity, while Luther's answer, or the Catholic Church's answer, has declined. As a result, we are, largely, Epicureans rather than Christians in the West today.

We should point out that, technically, Epicurus wasn't an atheist, as he maintained that the gods themselves were made of (very small) atoms ("god is an indestructible and blessed animal") and were, he assured readers, completely unconcerned with the affairs of men.[6] So Epicurus maintained, but most took him to be cloaking his atheism with faux piety in order to avoid the fate of Socrates who was executed by the Athenians on charges of unbelief. I note this because many Epicureans before, during, and after the

Reformation, exhibited the same faux piety in order to avoid persecution in a still-Christian society. (The distant god of the Deists, blithely unconcerned with human affairs, became the new and improved Epicurean deity, allowing for the faux piety of the Enlightenment.)

To return to the doctrines of Epicurus, as to this life, since we're only bodily creatures and there's only one life to live, our only goals are maximizing our pleasures or minimizing our pains. Epicurus himself opted for minimizing our pains through minimizing our pleasures, so as to avoid indigestion, hangovers, political entanglements, and woman troubles. But his followers chose maximizing pleasures through (clever lads) maximizing pleasures.[7] Thus, Epicureanism became the foundation for modern hedonism or libertinism, which of course proved a doubly attractive philosophy for those released from any worry about hell and damnation. "Eat, drink, and be sexually merry, for tomorrow your atoms might dissipate."

If anything, Epicurus' Roman disciple Lucretius was even more influential[8] because his philosophical poem *De Rerum Natura* was more bluntly anti-religious and crafted specifically to release men trapped "under the oppressive weight of religion."[9]

Lucretius intended his poem "to untie the knots of religion on the mind"[10] and to "cast down religion under foot."[11] Materialism is our freedom, he proclaimed, because "religion is the very thing that gives birth to wickedness and impious deeds."[12] Lucretius gave the example of Iphigenia, the young virgin girl offered by her father Agamemnon as a human sacrifice to soothe the offended goddess Artemis. But the same anti-religious sentiments were transferred, by the new devotees of Lucretius, to Christianity, which was scorned as an equally irrational, oppressive, and iniquitous faith.

Critics of Christianity, then and now, endlessly repeat a Lucretian phrase, *tantum religio potuit suadere malorum*, which translates roughly as, "such is the great amount of evil things religion is able to persuade men to do."[13] To ensure devotees were thoroughly liberated, Lucretius devoted an entire book of his six-book poem into dispelling any notion that the gods will be racking us in retribution after we die. We are only atoms that dissipate upon death. We have nothing to fear: "no one is handed over to the black abyss of Tartarus," because there is no such thing, and so no horrifying tortures await anyone—death is just extinction.[14]

What a boon. Death saves us from eternal life. Moreover, since we are merely atoms, and atoms are inert and lifeless, we aren't really alive anyway—what we call "life" is merely a transitory combination of lifeless atoms in a purposeless, godless cosmos. Pope John Paul II famously campaigned for a culture of life against a culture of death. We see in Epicurus and Lucretius and the famous pagan "despair" of the ancient world and the anxieties and demographic death-swirl of modern secularism, just how anti-life atheism really is.

Lucretius offered another entire book to describe how everything, from planets and stars to plants, animals, and humans, can be explained by the random interaction of atoms over infinite time.[15] His chance-governed, materialist creation story provided an entirely godless account of the evolution of living things nineteen centuries before Darwin. In fact, it was even before Luther's time, and was widely known throughout Europe two centuries before Darwin put pen to paper. Darwin's grandfather, Erasmus Darwin, used Lucretius as a source for his own evolutionary writings.

But Epicurus and Lucretius were not the only pagans resurrected to fight against the faith in the Renaissance. Another influential ancient atheist was Lucian of Samosata (125–180), a satirist and follower of Epicurus. In his dialogue *The Lover of Lies,* Lucian the skeptic dismisses the miraculous and supernatural, appealing to the atomism of Democritus, the Greek materialist "grandfather" of Epicurus.[16] He also made a direct hit against Christians in his satire *The Passing of Peregrinus,* wherein a Cynic philosopher, Peregrinus, briefly converts to Christianity as he flits from one apparently foolish superstition to another. Wandering through Palestine, Peregrinus comes upon the "wondrous wisdom of the Christians," and soon becomes a highly revered leader in his own right, "next after that other," Christ himself, "whom they still worship, the man who was crucified in Palestine because he introduced this new cult into the world."[17]

Peregrinus gets thrown in jail and makes the most out of it, milking the piety of the Christians who now regard him as a hero of the faith. So it was that "much money came to him from them by reason of his imprisonment, and he procured not a little revenue from it."[18]

Lucian describes Christians as "poor wretches" who accept religious "doctrines...without any definite evidence" and stupidly believe, against the wisdom of Epicurus, that "they are going to be immortal and live for all time...by worshipping that crucified sophist himself and living under his laws."[19]

Beyond these Epicureans, there were other ancient pagan sources of modern unbelief around at the time of Luther. There was also—strange to say it—the great Roman orator, statesman, and philosopher Cicero (106–43 BC). While Christians had affirmed Cicero's more popular, public Stoic side, which praised virtue and piety in such works as *De Re Publica* (*On the Republic*) and *De Officiis* (*On Duties*), Cicero was actually, as a philosopher, a kind of skeptic, who in other works that Christians had largely ignored, like *De Natura Deorum* (*On the Nature of the Gods*), *De Divinatione* (*On Divination*), and *Academica* (*On Academic Skepticism*), provided wonderfully witty and trenchant attacks on Greek and Roman religion. In the fifteenth through the eighteenth centuries, these attacks were repurposed and redirected at Christianity.

That's not the end of it. The rediscovery of the skeptical writings of Sextus Empiricus (AD 160–210) that attacked any notion of real certainty aided the modern atheist cause, as did, oddly enough, the writings of ancient historians like Polybius (200–118 BC), Livy (59 BC–AD 17), and Plutarch (AD 46–120). These pagan historians were not so much the enemies of ancient Greek or Roman religion, as they were skeptics of all religions; they took the attitude that clever philosopher-rulers had *invented* religions to keep the irrational and unruly masses obedient and orderly. The most effective way of controlling political subjects, Livy noted, is "putting into them the dread of the gods," which might require that one should "feign some miracle,"[20] or (as Plutarch reported) "pretend to have a vision from the god...."[21] If society, "could be composed of wise men," Polybius asserted, there would be no reason to create such "invisible terrors" as the fear of the gods or of Hades, but since the great masses of men are not rational, such useful fictions will always be necessary. Therefore, "those who now cast out these things are most rash and irrational."[22] Smart atheists know how to *use* the religion they secretly reject, including smart atheists living in cultures dominated by Christianity many centuries later.

This was an idea that, oddly enough, also entered the Christian West through Islam even earlier. The twelfth-century Islamic philosopher Averroes (Ibn Rushd, 1126–1198), whose commentaries on Aristotle were widely read in medieval Europe, likewise advanced the idea of the political utility of religion. Averroes put forth the so-called "double truth," the idea that there was the truth of philosophers (like Aristotle) and the truth of Koranic revelation. While Averroes, for reasons of self-preservation, placed Allah above the philosophers publicly, it is clear that this was the reverse of the actual hierarchy of his hidden beliefs: philosophers (like himself) were at the top (because they use their reason and can know the truth), and religious believers were at the bottom (because they are incapable of reason, and must be controlled by salutary religious myths invented by clever philosophers).[23] Thus, Averroes duplicated the pagan advice of Polybius, Livy, and Plutarch as applied to Islam.

Averroes' carefully worded philosophical skepticism was influential in the West long before the Reformation. By the thirteenth century, there were already "radical Aristotelians," such as Siger of Brabant (1240–1284), who were really Averroists who put rational philosophy above Christian revelation.

There is much more to this story, but for our purposes here, suffice it to say that by very early on, in some cases the 1200s and 1300s, there were those who began to be convinced that *all* religions, including Christianity, were actually false, but that some religions could be useful for the savvy statesmen. Machiavelli, a contemporary of Luther, would be the most powerful proponent of this view.

Ironically, it was the Catholic Church that through its system of universities contributed to the spread of these pagan and atheist ideas by debating them and stating them in detail (in printed books) in order to refute them. As Nicholas Davidson notes, "all the arguments necessary for a fully developed atheism were put into circulation by believers."[24] But we must not overlook the obvious: unbelievers were doing their share as well; otherwise, no one would have considered a debate to be necessary.

Atheism in Renaissance Italy

We can see why the Catholic Church in Rome would have been at the center of the debates about atheism. The origin of the Renaissance was Italy; and Italy thus became, through the rediscovery of pagan philosophy, the center of skepticism, though it often traveled, there and elsewhere, incognito in order to avoid the rebuke of Church authorities.[25] Hence, as Davidson informs us, "The conviction that Italy was a breeding-ground for atheists was...commonplace in the early modern period, especially among foreign visitors to the Peninsula."[26] In the middle of the 1500s, one such visitor, the English scholar and one-time tutor to Queen Elizabeth I, Roger Ascham, declared that in Italy "a man may freelie discourse against what he will, against whom he lust: against any Prince, against any gouernement, yea against God him selfe, and his whole Religion."[27] This Italian freedom to "discourse against what he will" was enough to convince many Protestants that Catholics were really pagans in thin disguise.

Among those Italians suspected of atheism were humanist philosopher Poggio Bracciolini (1380–1459) who rediscovered and circulated the text of Lucretius' *De Rerum Natura*; priest and educator Lorenzo Valla (1407–1457) who, along with debunking the "Donation of Constantine," wrote an infamous treatise, *De Voluptate*, in praise of Epicurean pleasure; philosopher and physician Pietro Pomponazzi (1462–1525) who doubted whether reason could prove the immortality of the soul; the pornographically inclined satirist Pietro Aretino (1492–1556); the Franciscan Friar turned Protestant Bernardino Ochino (1487–1564) who doubted the Holy Trinity and affirmed polygamy; the materialist philosopher Cesare Cremonini (1550–1631) who denied the existence of the immaterial soul; and the Epicurean materialist philosopher Lucilio Vanini (1585–1619) who is known as the father of modern libertinism. In addition to these, the famous Galileo was suspected of atheism because of his adherence to pagan Democritan atomism,[28] and there were not a few who thought that Pope Alexander VI was a secret unbeliever because of his openly impious life.[29] Finally, we may add to the list the scholar and philosopher Marsilius of Padua (1275–1342) and Italy's most famous atheist, Niccolò Machiavelli (1469–1527), both of whom we'll give closer treatments in a later chapter.

In 1513, Pope Leo X lamented at the Fifth Lateran Council that "in our days (which we endure with sorrow) the sower of cockle, the ancient enemy of the human race, has dared to scatter and multiply in the Lord's field some extremely pernicious errors, which have always been rejected by the faithful, especially on the nature of the rational soul, with the claim that it is mortal...[I]t is our desire to apply suitable remedies against this infection and, with the approval of the sacred council, we condemn and reject all those who insist that the intellectual soul is mortal.... For the soul not only truly exists of itself...but it is also immortal...."[30] The real target of his condemnation: Epicureans.

Who's to Blame?

So, who was at fault for Italy's very early, very wayward ways? We can begin an answer by asking, whom did they blame *at the time?* "The origins of Italian atheism were variously traced [in the late 1400s and the 1500s]: to the new learning of the Renaissance or the survival of scholasticism; to the Lutheran Reformation or the influence of Catholicism; to the Calvinists or the Anabaptists; to the disciples of Machiavelli or the followers of Epicurus."[31]

That's an interesting mixture of pre-Reformation and Reformation causes. In one way or another, most were reasonable conjectures. We've already seen the contents of the new learning, focused on the revival of pagan literature, including Epicurus. Likewise, since Catholic scholasticism was rooted in a deep appreciation of Aristotle, Averroism often came with it, and so it seemed as if Catholicism were a conduit for Averroism. In addition, clearly Alexander VI gave the distinct impression that an unbeliever sat on the throne of St. Peter.

But Protestants did not escape blame. Lutheranism, which trumpeted that faith and not works saved, was thereby thought by its enemies to foster immoral antinomianism (lawlessness) and hence sexual license or Epicurean hedonism (even though Luther himself adamantly attacked those who steered his theology in that direction). Some Calvinists actually embraced antinomianism, and hence were thought to represent a new form of Epicurean. Anabaptists were, as we'll see below, often on the forefront of the most radical Reformation thought that bore a curious resemblance to anti-Christian thought. Of course, Epicurus and Machiavelli speak for themselves.

This mixture of suspected causes at the dawn of the Reformation is illuminating. It allows us to see how the battles of the Reformation fit into the advance of modern atheism. Let me provide two interesting examples.

The Venetian Council of Ten was charged with overseeing the Republic of Venice. In 1533, it ordered the city of Verona to clamp down on the corrupt friars at San Fermo. These friars, thundered the Council, "do not want to live under the rule of their founder, but as sons of iniquity...as Epicureans and Lutherans." Thus we can see that, to Catholics at least, Luther's doctrine of justification by faith alone seemed to imply Epicurean hedonism, "Do whatever you want, because you're saved by faith anyway!"

Another example comes from the Anabaptists, who were among the most radical of the Reformers animated by the doctrine of justification by faith alone, but using it to justify a radical redefinition of the faith. In 1550 there was a synod of Anabaptist radicals in Venice. The synod concluded that immaterial things such as the soul don't exist, that demons and angels therefore don't exist either, and that Jesus Christ was merely human and the natural son of Jesus and Mary. They also expressed doubt about the reliability of the Bible, a strange result of the Protestant focus on the Bible alone as *the* source of authority.[32]

And so, both Catholics and Protestants share the blame for aiding the cause of modern atheism. If papal corruption—and even Catholic learning and universities—can be held accountable for the spread of paganism and atheism, so too can Luther's doctrine of *sola scriptura*, which not only created a multitude of different Protestant variations based upon rival interpretations, but reinforced the existing skeptical notion that the Bible was not revealed truth, and that Christianity was entirely subjective—just as irrational as any ancient pagan religion. Some, like those radical Anabaptists, affirmed existing atheistic belief (by denying the divinity of Jesus) and others, like John Calvin with his doctrine that an inscrutable Christian God predestines some human beings to hell, affirmed the skeptics' turn to a Lucretius and his denial of divine judgment, which seemed more rational and humane than what the Christians had to offer.

But Christians should remember that even if the Reformation hadn't happened, the secular revolution had already begun. If there were no Protestants, then the Catholic Church would be the sole, battered survivor in the West today. But the Reformation did happen, and we must understand how the secular revolution used it to better achieve its aim of extinguishing Catholics and Protestants alike.

WHY İSLAM WAS İMPORTANT TO THE REFORMATION

We now turn to another extra-Christian aspect of the Reformation that, like the rise of atheism, is largely untouched in most histories of the period, the importance of Islam.

There are two very good reasons for examining Islam in a book about the Reformation. The first is that in our own time Islam represents an enormous threat to Christianity, and it isn't just the threat of jihad. Under a wave of Muslim immigration, Europe is being Islamicized at an unprecedented rate. Islam threatens to replace both secularism and Christianity (Catholic and Protestant) as *the* culture-defining, law-defining foundation of European civilization. The victory of Islam over Christian and secularized (i.e., de-Christianized) Europe will not then have occurred through jihad, but simply through the demographic displacement of Europeans. This displacement has occurred, largely, through the policies of secular liberal governments that have simultaneously actively de-Christianized their countries, advanced a sexual revolution that discourages childbearing, *and* then encouraged Islamic immigration to make up for alleged labor shortfalls or out of a multicultural belief that Islamic culture is as good as any other and Europe should accept as many immigrants as it can. In an Islamic Europe, it should go without saying (as history and current Islamic societies show us), Christians will be subordinated to Islamic rule.

The second reason may be something of a surprise. The same fear that Christians feel *today* at the advance of Islam, was felt even more keenly back *then*, at the time of Martin Luther. The fear of Islam was part of the general apocalyptic dread that gripped all the Reformation's participants, Catholic and Protestant. For Luther especially, Islam was seen as the scourge of an angry God, aimed at an unrepentant Europe.

We cannot understand the urgency of the Reformation in general, and Luther in particular, without understanding the effects of this apocalyptic fear. Many, including Luther, believed that they were in the last times, and that the advance of Islam signaled the final, great apocalyptic battle that would signal the end of the world as prophesied in the book of Revelation. This fear made it all the more believable that the pope was in fact the Antichrist, the great Whore of Babylon. It should then come as a bit of surprise to readers to find out that Luther ensured the publication of a new translation of the Koran, to which he provided a preface. Why? We shall find out below.

We may add a third reason to examine Islam as part of the Reformation. The contemporary Islamic takeover of Europe is due, in great part, to the dominance of secularism which simultaneously declares Christianity to be the worst of all religions, and welcomes Muslims as the best of all neighbors, *even though everything about Islam is diametrically opposed to secular liberalism*. As a result, one barely hears a peep from the secular left at the massive extermination of Christians now, but much about the horror of the Christian crusades against the allegedly innocent Muslims way back when.

This strange attitude of the secular Left isn't new, but has been part and parcel of modern European atheism from the late Middle Ages on; it wasn't just the ancient pagans who were considered superior to the Christian culture of Europe, so was just about every other culture, including most particularly Islamic culture which was simple and manly and permitted polygamy and had supposedly enjoyed its own period of glorious learning in the past. The view of European secularists has always been that *anything* is better than Judeo-Christianity, especially Islam. Now you know why the Left today seems to love Islam and despise Christianity, even at the cost of its own self-destruction.

A Short Primer on Islam

Christians are generally confused about Islam—not just the Left—so a brushing up is necessary for us to understand the real situation with Islam in the Reformation (and now, as well).

First of all, Islam is not based only on the Koran, the holy book of Islam, in the way that Protestantism is based upon the Old and New Testaments. Islam actually has three other sources of divine revelation at its foundation, the Torah given by God to Moses, the Psalms given to David, and the Injil (Gospel) given to Issa (Jesus).[1] This last is not the Christian New Testament, however, but a different version that no longer exists.

We do find, in the Koran, some account of Jesus's birth and life that shows obvious knowledge of the Gospel accounts,[2] but there are also significant differences. So while Gabriel announces the miraculous virgin birth of Jesus to Mary,[3] and Jesus does work miracles, his divinely ordained mission as the Messiah is to prepare the way for Muhammad,[4] the final prophet, who brings the final revelation, the Koran.[5] Moreover, Jesus was not crucified, but according to the Koran he was raised bodily into heaven by Allah.[6] Interestingly enough, Jesus will return as a kind of sign of the final judgment, but as a subordinate to Muhammad.[7]

In Islam, Jesus is *not* the son of God, and the Koran explicitly rejects the Holy Trinity. (Muslims, like Jews, reject the Holy Trinity because they believe that it violates the unity of one God.) In fact, the Koran has Jesus himself deny his divinity.[8]

This is key to understanding Islam's relationship to Judaism and Christianity. Since both Jews and Christians had the truth revealed to them, and then rejected the fullness of revelation as it is found in the Koran as revealed to Muhammad, they are infidels (*kafir*). Infidels are different from pagans, who have not had any revelation at all. Infidel Jews and Christians *refuse to see* that the Torah, Psalms, and the (lost) Gospel all point to Muhammad as the final prophet and the Koran as the final revealed text. Muslims therefore firmly believe that Allah decrees that divine punishments await those Jews and Christians who reject Muhammad and the Koran. Moreover, because Christians believe in the Holy Trinity, they are guilty of the worst kind of infidelity, committing the only unforgivable sin in Islam, *shirk*: the deification of anyone other than Allah.[9]

In addition to the Koran, the Torah, the Psalms, and the lost Gospel about Jesus, Muslims look to the authority of the *Hadiths*, the various collections of the deeds and sayings of Muhammad as reported by others. The *Hadiths* are not a short collection, but an extensive multi-volume compendium of nearly every aspect of Muhammad's life, down to the seemingly most trivial details. Given the sheer volume of *Hadiths*, and the task of connecting them to the Koran, there arose scholars within Islam, the *imams*, who provide the consensus of authoritative interpretation.[10]

The *Hadiths* guide Muslims in two important ways. First, Muhammad's life and sayings in the *Hadiths* define the proper interpretation of the Koran (via the consensus of the *imams*).[11] Second, Muhammad's life in the *Hadiths* shows the orthodox *exactly* how they should live, down to the smallest details, and that obviously includes how to spread Islam.

Muhammad and Jihad

The difference between Christianity and Islam can be readily discerned by comparing the lives of their founders. Jesus preached turning the other cheek, loving enemies, and accepting persecution in imitation of his own impending crucifixion. Muhammad was a prophet-warrior, who gained control of the Arabian Peninsula through force of arms, imposing Islam on its inhabitants in an estimated eighty-two battles. For Islam in any age, conquest is an imitation of its founder, and conquest is holy war, jihad.

There have been many attempts (generally by the Left) to soften jihad, as if it could be reduced to "missionary zeal," but the truth remains: from the beginning, conquest was central to Islam, not an aberration of it.[12]

Muhammad died in AD 632, leaving no clearly designated successor (or caliph). The two great branches of Islam, Sunni and Shi'a, arise from the dispute about who is the proper successor to the prophet. Sunnis chose Abu Bakr, a friend and advisor of Muhammad as well as the father of one of his wives, Aisha. The Shi'a chose Muhammad's cousin and son-in-law, Ali. Sunnis assert that the best successor should be chosen as caliph, Shi'a that the successor should be related to Muhammad.

Establishing oneself as Muhammad's successor is essential to setting up the political-religious rule of Islam, the caliphate. The designated caliph has something of the status of the pope for Roman Catholics, except there is no distinction of mosque and state for Muslims, so it would be more like a fusion of pope and emperor. The unity of the caliphate provides the geographical-political-theological starting point for the unity of Muslims worldwide, and therefore, their universal goal of conquering the world for Allah and the establishment of Islam. All national boundaries are arbitrary and temporary, and destined to be replaced by a world-wide caliphate.

This universal goal is achieved in the same way that Muhammad conquered the Arabian Peninsula, by war that gives the conquered three choices: convert to Islam, or pay the tax levied on unbelievers, or die. In the Koran we find, "Fight those who do not believe in Allah or in the Last Day and who do not consider unlawful what Allah and His Messenger have made unlawful and who do not adopt the religion of truth from those who were given the Scripture—[fight] until they give the *jizya* [tax on non-Muslims] willingly while they are humbled."[13] In one of the *Hadiths*, we find the authoritative extension of this principle. Muhammad is reported to have said to his officers,

> Fight in the name of Allah and in the way of Allah. Fight against those who disbelieve in Allah. Make a holy war [jihad],...When you meet your enemies who are polytheists [Christians included, because of their belief in the Holy Trinity], invite them to three courses of action...invite them to [accept] Islam; if they respond to you, accept it from them and desist from fighting against them.... If they refuse to accept Islam, demand from them the *jizya*. If they agree to pay, accept it from them and hold off your hands. If they refuse to pay the tax, seek Allah's help and fight them.[14]

In another of the *Hadiths*, we find the following (as narrated Abdullah bin Masud):

> I asked Allah's Apostle [i.e., Muhammad], "O Allah's Apostle! What is the best deed?" He replied, "To offer the prayers at their early stated fixed times." I asked, "What is next in goodness?" He replied, "To be good and dutiful to your parents." I further asked, what is next in goodness?" He replied, "To participate in Jihad in Allah's Cause."[15]

And in yet another *Hadith*, we see that the universal aim of Islam must be achieved through conquest:

> Allah's Apostle [Muhammad] said, "I have been ordered to fight with the people till they say, 'None has the right

to be worshipped but Allah,' and whoever says, 'None has the right to be worshipped but Allah,' his life and property will be saved by me except for Islamic law, and his accounts will be with Allah, (either to punish him or to forgive him.)"[16]

Thus, the aim was not simply conquest and conversion, but the subjection of the unconverted populace in what is called *dhimmitude*, the *dhimmi* being the non-Islamic population. This subjection, in turn, became an essential source of revenue, through the payment of the *jizya*, which supported the conquering Muslims.[17]

Jihad and the Spread of Islam into Christendom

In Islam's first three centuries (600–900), it spread west from the Arabian Peninsula across north Africa into Spain, as well as north and east through the Holy Land to India. It was spread not by conversion but (as Muhammad had conquered and unified Arabia) by war, the sword of conquest. And we must not forget that, with the exception of India, these were largely Christian-dominated lands.

War against Christians is part of the Koran's antagonism toward all non-believers: "And fight them until there is no *fitnah* [worship of other gods than Allah] and [until] the religion, all of it, is for Allah."[18] The Koran even implies that unbelievers are not only contemptible but irredeemable: "Indeed, the worst of living creatures in the sight of Allah are those who have disbelieved, and they will not [ever] believe...."[19] The true believers are urged to holy war, knowing that Allah will be always on their side, even if outnumbered.[20]

So, as one would expect, Christians fell by the sword as Islam spread.[21] In the seventh century, Christians were slaughtered in Syria, monasteries were sacked and pillaged in Mesopotamia, the towns of Behnesa, Fayum, Nikiu, and Aboit in Egypt were put to the sword, Cilicia was taken into captivity, the people of Euchaita in Armenia were destroyed, Cyprus was sacked, Tripoli pillaged, Chalcedon taken, and Carthage wiped out.[22] Jerusalem fell to the Muslims in 637. And that was just the beginning.

The expansion of Islam continued for several centuries. In the eighth century, Spain was conquered, and the invading Muslims reached Tours in north-central France in 732, captured Arles, Narbonne, Beziers, Montpellier, Nimes, and Marseille. The caliph's general, Musa bin Nusayr, thought Europe was in his grasp.

> With powerful armament by sea and land he was preparing to re-cross the Pyrenees, to extinguish Gaul and Italy, the declining kingdoms of the Franks and Lombards, and to preach the unity of God on the altar of the Vatican. From there, subduing the Barbarians of Germany, he proposed to follow the course of the Danube from its source to the Euxine Sea, to overthrow... Constantinople, and returning to Asia, to unite his new acquisitions with Antioch and the Provinces of Syria.[23]

In the ninth century, Muslims attacked Sicily, and they nearly entered Rome in 846, damaging the churches of St. Peter and St. Paul (leaving only because Pope Leo IV promised them money).

They pillaged Campagna in Italy in 876, and burned the monastery of Mount Cassio to the ground in 884.

By the beginning of the tenth century, the Muslim conquest of Sicily was complete, they controlled all passes in the Alps between France and Italy, and reached Toulouse. On Palm Sunday 937, Jerusalem was attacked, and Muslims burnt down several churches after pillaging them.

In the eleventh century, they conquered Armenia and Antioch, and began settling between the Danube and the Balkans. They burned down the Church of the Holy Sepulchre in Jerusalem in 1009, a repeat of previous Muslim destruction in 614 and 966. The Fatimid caliph al-Hakim not only destroyed thousands of churches, but he demanded that Christians and Jews wear black turbans, and in addition, that Christians wear a large wooden cross and Jews a wooden block in the shape of a calf to remind them of their idolatry.[24] Campaigns of jihad up and down the Holy Land caused incredible destruction, including the slaughter of three thousand inhabitants of Jerusalem.[25]

In 1453, the Muslim armies of the Ottoman Turks captured Constantinople, and turned one of the oldest and most beautiful churches in Christendom, Hagia Sophia, into a mosque. Muslim armies besieged Vienna in 1529 (and again in 1683). It wasn't until 1571, at the giant naval battle of Lepanto, that the Muslim attempt to dominate Mediterranean Europe was miraculously foiled, though the Islamic threat remained for more than another century.

What about the Crusades?

Readers will note that I didn't mention the Crusades. That's because the Crusades, beginning at the end of the eleventh century and undertaken by Christians to recover the Holy Land, were, in this broad history, a very minor setback in the ongoing expansion of Islam from the time of Muhammad up until the sixteenth century.

We say minor because, while the first Crusade established a short-lived Crusader kingdom in the Holy Land, the Crusades as a whole made barely a dent in Islam. As historian Efraim Karsh makes abundantly clear, during this period Islam was absorbed in its own internecine warfare between the Shiite Fatimid dynasty and the Sunni Abbasid dynasty. "They feared and loathed each other as much as they feared and loathed the Christian powers, and this precluded any conceivable collaboration between them against the European invaders" in the Holy Land.[26]

The Christian incursion of the Crusades was therefore a momentary episode in Islam's own history of successful conquering of Christian territory, and "affected only a fraction of the Middle East.... As a result, the crusades were seen not as a cataclysmic event but as yet another round in the intermittent fighting that had been raging between the Byzantine and the Islamic empires for centuries," as Islam pressed upon Christian domains from the east. "There was no general fear of impending doom to Islam's collective existence, and the Muslim dynasts and potentates viewed the crusades in purely localized terms."[27] When the Christians did make some small headway, the Islamic leaders were largely inclined to work them into the shifting alliances and antagonisms among Muslims already in the region, "based on the vicissitudes in the regional balance of forces and opportunities rather than on religious affiliation, which as often as not pitted Muslim and Christian against Muslim and Christian."[28]

Given this larger context, it's clear that Christianity had experienced a hammering by Islam for about five hundred years prior to the Crusades, and had lost much of its original Christianized territory around the Mediterranean. The momentary and minimal incursion of the Crusades was soon erased, and Islamic expansion continued for the next several centuries. Thus, from the Christian perspective at the time of the Reformation, it was entirely conceivable that Islam could again besiege Rome.

Islam and the Reformation

The caliphate that vexed Europe in the 1400s and 1500s was that of the Ottoman Empire founded by Osman Bey (or Osman Gazi or Ottoman) at the end of the thirteenth century in what today is Turkey. Ottoman "society was dominated by the distinct militant ethos of the *ghaza,* or holy war, reminiscent of Islam's earliest days, which combined the love of fighting and its spoils—booty, territory, and prestige—with unwavering religious commitment to world conquest through perpetual raiding and colonization of infidel dominions."[29]

The militant Ottomans were settled not far from Constantinople, and surrounded it over the course of the next century until on May 29, 1453, the Ottoman sultan "Mehmed II rode his white horse into Constantinople, making this proud city his new imperial capital and winning the honorific title of 'The Conqueror.'"[30] Efraim Karsh continues, "For the West this was a dark moment. For Islam it was a cause for celebration. For nearly a millennium Constantinople had been the foremost barrier—both physically and ideologically—to Islam's sustained drive for world conquest and the object of desire of numerous Muslim rulers." With this conquest, the Ottoman sultan Mehmed became "the head of a great empire stretching from the Black Sea to the very heart of Europe and the legitimate heir to the universal Byzantine Empire."[31]

The Ottoman advance was not finished. By the time that he died in 1481, Mehmed "had completed the conquest of Greece, Serbia, and the Balkan territories south of the Danube, and had added the Crimean Peninsula to his domains...." His grandson took the Levant and Egypt, and his great grandson, Iraq, North Africa, most of Hungary "and established a foothold in southern Italy. In 1529, the Ottomans were knocking at the gates of Vienna. Even in remote Iceland the Lutheran Book of Common Prayer pleaded to God Almighty to save the people from 'the terror of the Turk.'"[32]

To Pope Leo X and the Holy Roman Emperor Charles V, Luther's protests and rebellion were a distraction from what really mattered, which was preventing the Ottoman Turks from conquering Europe. Leo had called for a Crusade against the invaders and Charles was fighting them. The Muslims invaded Hungary in 1521 (where Charles' brother-in-law Louis was king; Louis was killed in battle in 1526) and besieged Vienna in 1529. To pope and emperor, Islam was a real and present danger that needed to be fought. Luther had other ideas.

Luther and Islam

In 1518—remarking on his own *Ninety-Five Theses*—Martin Luther asserted, "To fight against the Turk is the same as resisting God, who visits our sin upon us with this rod."[33] This reaction of Luther's is, perhaps, more understandable in terms of his general view, rooted in Scripture, that Christians must be obedient to civil authorities. But it is also true that he considered Turkish aggression as a punishment for papal sin. In an odd way, then, the Islamic threat confirmed Luther's own aims. Scholars Sarah Henrich and James Boyce elaborate:

> In his later *On War against the Turk* of 1529, Luther used similar language [as he had elsewhere], describing the Turk as "the rod of God's wrath" by which "God is punishing the world." This conviction led him to call for leaders who would exhort the people "to repentance and prayer" because "we have earned God's wrath and disfavor, so that he justly gives us into the hands of the devil and the Turk." Such a view was repeated in various ways but essentially unchanged in Luther's numerous comments and correspondence and in his major published pieces about "the Turks" from 1528 through 1542.[34]

To point out the obvious, this made Luther appear to be suggesting that the way to meet the Islamic advance was humble submission, which further alienated his cause in the eyes of the papacy and the emperor. *On War against the Turk* was actually Luther's attempt to clarify his position, and answer the charge of aiding and abetting the Muslim cause. Luther did see the Muslim advance as an agent of God's wrath against Church corruption, but he also made clear that the proper Christian authority should wage war—in this case (ironically) the proper authority was the very Catholic Charles V, Holy Roman Emperor, against whom Luther himself was pitted theologically and politically. This war should be defensive, rather than a crusade to eliminate Islam. To this last point, Luther added an impolitic dig, that if Charles V really desired "to destroy unbelievers and non-Christians, he would have to begin with the pope, bishops, and clergy, and perhaps not spare us or himself."[35]

We don't want to misrepresent Luther. His attitude toward Islam was not irenic, to say the least. According to Luther, the dreaded Turk is a "destroyer, enemy and blasphemer of our Lord Jesus Christ, a man who instead of the gospel and faith sets up his shameful Muhammad and all kinds of lies, ruins all temporal government and home life or marriage, and his warfare, which is nothing but murder and bloodshed, is a tool of the devil himself."[36] However, Luther tossed Catholics and Muslims into the same category, writing that Muslims "deny and ardently persecute Christ, no less than our papists deny and persecute him."[37]

The way to take on Islam, Luther asserted, was actually through knowledge of its doctrines, not just by the sword. He believed that Islam had been misrepresented, and that it was necessary to reassess it more honestly. This was all the more important because—and this is a key point—in Luther's view *Muslims were actually morally and ceremonially superior to Christians*:

> The religion of the Turks or Muhammad is far more splendid in ceremonies—and, I might almost say, in customs—than ours, even including that of the religious or all the clerics. The modesty and simplicity of their food, clothing, dwellings, and everything else, as well as the fasts, prayers, and common gatherings of the people... are nowhere seen among us.... Furthermore, which of our monks, be it a Carthusian (they who wish to appear the best) or a Benedictine, is not put to shame by the miraculous and wondrous abstinence and discipline

among their religious? Our religious are mere shadows when compared to them, and our people clearly profane when compared to theirs.[38]

The superiority of Christianity lay not in ceremonial splendor or in moral action (or works) but in the acceptance of the gospel as Luther understood it, which justified man by faith alone.

Therefore, Luther's strategy, if we may call it that, was to promote an understanding of Islam, and use this knowledge as a means to help undermine the papacy. In fact, Luther argued, "the papists actually sought to conceal the truth about the Muslim religion so that it might not be revealed how similar was their own perversion of Christianity, and that they might avoid having to refute things that their actions showed them to approve."[39]

Luther was therefore determined to ensure that the Koran was available and widely disseminated. As a result, a new translation of the Koran was published in 1543, with a preface by Dr. Martin Luther and fellow reformer Philip Melanchthon. In the preface, Luther states,

I do not doubt that the more other pious and learned persons read these writings, the more the errors and the name of Muhammad will be refuted. For just as the folly, or rather madness, of the Jews is more easily observed once their hidden secrets have been brought out into the open, so once the book of Muhammad has been made public and thoroughly examined in all its parts, all pious persons will more easily comprehend the insanity and wiles of the devil and will be more easily able to refute them. This is the reason that has moved me to wish to publish this book.[40]

The comment about the Jews is important, because Luther was deeply anti-Semitic, seeing the Jews as the predecessors to the papists in pushing ceremonies and works-righteousness.[41] Sadly, he may have found kindred notions in the violently anti-Jewish passages of the Koran.[42] In any case, Luther believed that publication of the Koran was part of his effort to repel all his enemies, not just the Ottoman Turks.

> This must not be thought a matter of light importance, especially by those of us who teach in the church. We must fight on all fronts against the ranks of the devil. In this age of ours how many varied enemies have we already seen? Papist defenders of idolatry, the Jews, the multifarious monstrosities of the Anabaptists, Servetus, and others. Let us now prepare ourselves against Muhammad.[43]

Thus, according to Luther, the fight against Islam was just part of his larger fight against the papists, the Jews, and even the Protestants with whom he disagreed.

Other Protestant Reformers and Islam

Other Protestant reformers, who disagreed with Luther theologically, agreed with him that Muslims and Catholics were equally bad.[44] John Calvin thought Muslims were a heretical sect (like the

Arians) rather than a different religion, though the Muslim caliph and the pope were both Antichrists, two horns of the demonic beast in Daniel.[45] "In many of Calvin's writings we find that his commentary on the Turks was really an occasion to vent his obvious criticism of Roman Catholics (often referred to simply as 'the Papists')."[46]

So, for example, we find the following in one of Calvin's sermons on Genesis, which echoes Luther's lumping together of Judaism, Catholicism, and Islam: "The Turks, the Jews and the Papists abuse this holy name [of God], going so far as to sully it, as the Turks who adore what they fabricate in their brains and blaspheme (in this way) the living God."[47] Or this, from Calvin's commentary on Ephesians: "As for the Turks, they will say again and again, 'God Almighty,' creator of heaven and earth. The Papists protest quite often that they believe in God just as do the Turks and Jews. But the Papists fight against the truth."[48]

An interesting picture of the time can be glimpsed in the following. After the Catholic Emperor Charles V had prescribed regular prayer days against the Turks, "In 1541 Reformed [Calvinist] preachers in Strasbourg and Geneva urged the city magistrates to introduce similar days of prayer and penitence. The prayer used in Geneva was included in the introduction to Calvin's sermons on Jeremiah and Lamentations. Part of that reads: '(Lord), do not allow that those should perish over whom according to thine holy will thy name was invoked, and that the Turks, pagans, papists and other unbelievers would glorify while blaspheming thee.'"[49]

Calvin did rightly understand that all Christians would suffer if the Ottoman Turks succeeded in their efforts. In Jan Slomp's assessment, "Calvin realized that if the Turks were to conquer all of Europe it would be the end of Christianity as a power to be reckoned with. 'The danger exists that there will be a greater bar-barity in Christianity than ever before,' he observed in sermon 28 on Daniel 11:30–32, 'because the Turk will be able to gain every-thing. After that, he will cause Christianity to be abolished to such an extent that there will be no memory left of it.'"[50]

So, in sum, while Catholics saw Islam as an age-old antagonist, and one that should unify Christendom in opposition, Protestants saw Islam as simply another heresy like Catholicism, one as bad as the other, except that Islam might very well succeed in the exter-mination of Christianity.

The Pagan View of Islam at the Time of the Reformation

The philosophical pagans of the Reformation era and the Radical Enlightenment sided more with Luther than with the pope, but for reasons of their own. In principle, they believed all religion was superstition. But in order to more effectively unseat Catholicism in particular, and Christianity in general, from its privileged cultural position, they asserted that Islam was actually superior morally and even theologically, the latter because it was more Deist-friendly (that is anti-Trinitarian). Some thought it had political advantages too.

So while some atheists and Deists hammered Islam with the same vigor that they hammered Christianity, Jonathan Israel notes, "By and large...antipathy yielded in radical texts to an image of Islam as a pure monotheism of high moral caliber which was also a revolutionary force for positive change and one which from the outset proved to be both more rational and less bound to the mirac-ulous than Christianity or Judaism."[51] Many atheist- or deist-leaning philosophers[52] also believed that Islam had spread so quickly, not by the sword (as ignoble Christians falsely maintained), but by the fact that it was so tolerant, rational, and benevolent that Christian populations ran to embrace the Islamic advance.[53] The Crusades, in this radical revisionist view, were not an attempt to protect Christianity from invasion, but a typical warmongering attack by morally inferior Christians upon peaceful Muslims.[54] Islam (not Christianity), these free thinkers argued, had been the real bearer of reason through the Dark Ages, with the Muslim philosopher Averroes being the great sign of the essential nobility of the Muslim over the Christian world. Even more surprising, they asserted the deepest *philosophic* wisdom was actually carried forth by an allegedly clandestine cadre of Islamic philosophers within the Ottoman Empire, the very empire that had almost crushed Europe during the century of the Reformation.[55]

That this was all unhistorical hooey has not prevented it from being accepted in attitude, if not necessarily in its particulars, by atheistic secular liberalism today. So while early Reformation-era Catholics saw Islam as *the* great threat against Europe, and Protestants saw it as another heresy like Catholicism, secular-minded liberals then (and now) saw it not as it actually was but simply as another instrument, even ally, in their effort to crush the Christian civilization they both depend on and purport to scorn.

CHAPTER SEVEN

A Large Part of the Reformation Was Driven by Nationalism

There are many studies of the Reformation as primarily a religious phenomenon, since it obviously concerns fundamental disputes about theological doctrines and the proper structure of the Church. While this is certainly important, and we'll come to that soon enough, if we don't understand the political context of the Reformation period, we'll not understand why it turned out the way it did.

At the time of the Reformation, the politics of western Europe were divided between the imperial aims of the Holy Roman Emperor and the localized aims of national kings and territorial princes, with the pope a territorial prince as well as universal spiritual leader. Roughly speaking, what happened during the Reformation was that kings and princes invoked Protestantism to assert their independence while the Empire invoked Catholicism as an instrument of imperial policy. Some knowledge of these various players is therefore necessary to understand why what are often taken as theological controversies and conflicts were often more political than religious.

The Occasionally Holy and Not Actually Roman Emperors, German Elector Princes, and Princely Popes

We may call Constantine the first Holy Roman Emperor because he's the first of the Christian emperors, but the honorary title is usually given to Pepin's son, Charles the Great, or Charlemagne (800–814), crowned by Pope Leo III as not just as King of the Franks but as *Imperator Romanorum*.

The Holy Roman Emperors were actually German, not Roman, and while the emperors came from dynastic houses—the Habsburgs during the Reformation—from very early on the Germanic nobles had elected their kings, and that tradition developed into a system of German nobles (Prince Electors) who did the actual choosing of the Holy Roman Emperor.

Long before the Reformation, the settled custom was to have seven Electors. They included three archbishops representing the most powerful ecclesiastical centers of the Germanic region (Mainz, Trier, Cologne) and four lay German nobles representing the most powerful ancient Germanic tribal areas (Bohemia, Palatine, Saxony, and Brandenburg).

The emperor often assumed the mantle of protector of the Church in his vast realm and the German emperors had, as we've seen, a history of reforming the papacy when it couldn't reform itself. Thus, while the emperor often regarded the pope as an ally, he could also regard him as a subordinate bishop when it came to politics and the Church of Rome as a subordinate estate Church. That was not the papacy's view of course. The Church claimed universal spiritual authority and, as we've seen in our chapter on the Papal States, the popes had their own political and territorial concerns which often tainted the purity of their motives.

There was also the issue of money. The emperor could not always count on the German nobles providing enough of it to run the Empire, so he would turn to the coffers of Rome, since he did so much good work on behalf of the Church. The papacy, in turn, came up with an inventive way to finance its own operations—political and religious—namely, selling indulgences.[1] The protest against sale of indulgences, as is well known, was at the very center of Luther's famous *Ninety-Five Theses*. More on that later.

Nationalism and National Churches: France and England

Many kings of course resented having to tolerate a powerful independent (and arguably superior) institution like the Church operating within their realms but not under their control. So they tried various ways to bring their local churches to heel. This had been true for centuries, and had led to countless conflicts over lay investiture and other controversies between Church and political leaders.

It wouldn't be too far wrong to say that when Philip IV of France brought the papacy to Avignon that he established de facto the first national Church (albeit one that retained its universal claims). Simply put, Philip wanted his own *national* Church and he got it, what later came to be called the Gallican Church, the Church under control of the French monarch.

For Philip, a national Church was a dandy source of revenue to finance wars, and the Hundred Years' War between England and France that commenced two decades after his death was a major driver of nationalist feelings in the two countries, in which religion became a factor to justify each country's cause. The first Avignon pope, Clement V, extolled the French in 1311 to be "just like the Israelite people," that is a holy people, "elected by the Lord in execution of the mandates of heaven..."[2] Statements like that were excellent "nationalist" propaganda pieces when France took up war with England about a quarter century later.

England, as historian Michael Wilks points out, also claimed its cause was holy and "English political theology under royal patronage forged a most intimate connection between the Church and the land, between Eng-*land*, the national community, and the idea of the regional Church as an *ecclesia terrae Angliae*," the Church of the English land. By this fusion of Church and state, the English people were "the new chosen race, the heirs of the promised land."[3] And so (to use J. W. McKenna's apt phrase) "God became an Englishman," that is, the English in battling the French during the Hundred Years' War believed that *they*, and not the French, were God's chosen people and the instrument of God's purposes.[4]

One obvious eventual historical outcome of the Catholic Church in England becoming the *ecclesia terrae Angliae* was King Henry

VIII's Act of Supremacy pushed through Parliament in 1534. It boldly stated that "the King our Sovereign Lord, his heirs and successors, kings of this realm, shall be taken, accepted, and reputed the only Supreme Head on earth of the Church of England, called *Anglicana Ecclesia....*"[5] Henry VIII thus positioned himself, at least in his own mind and propaganda, less as a Protestant rebel than as a patriotic conservative reaffirming a long-standing English tradition, wherein the king, as ruler of his realm, also ruled the national Church free of foreign interference.

Germany's National Church

The situation in Germany was more complex. The German Elector Princes who chose the Holy Roman (really, German) Emperor also wanted to keep him on a very short leash. They didn't want the emperor to "dominate and reduce them to an obedience not dissimilar to that exercised by the King of France over his subjects."[6] If that weren't politically confusing enough, Germany was divided and subdivided into a confusing patchwork of lesser rulers, each of which strained against the others.

Even with their divisions into these various layers of princedoms and dukedoms, the Germans were united in their own long-standing national feud with the papacy, with German churches complaining that their revenues were being used to feather the pope-prince's nest at Rome. Witness this complaint from the Archbishop of Mainz, Germany, penned in 1457, more than fifty years *before* Luther's formal complaint against indulgences. The German Elector Archbishop complained that Pope Callixtus III (reign, 1455–1458) "despises the German nation and seems bent on sapping it of its strength and substance." He continued, "New indulgences are approved day after day for one purpose only: their profits to Rome." Then he declared rather boldly, "Now, however, our leaders have been, so to speak, awakened from their sleep and have begun to ponder what means they might take to oppose their misfortunes, shake off their yoke, and regain the ancient freedom they have lost. Consider what a blow it will be to Rome if the German princes should succeed in their design!"[7]

This was not an isolated instance. There was a political "tradition of complaint" by the Germans against Rome, and part of this tradition assumed that it would be better if Germany were like France and England, both of which had effectively established national Churches that could put their own interests first and keep church revenues local. This meant that "Desire for reform [in Germany] was...powerfully bound up with a desire for a national church,"[8] that is, reform was not solely a theological concern.

This was especially true because the papacy had become dominated by Italians, and in the century before Luther, it became popular among the Germans to think that the Germanic peoples were *more* ancient than Italians and the Romans, and hence superior. Indeed, the Germans (some claimed) were the descendants of Noah, the primal "ur-folk" tribe of Europe, and hence the appropriate seat of divine authority (not Rome). As one enthusiast stated, "God chose you [the Germans] before all others," and moreover, "gave you the monarchy of the world [the Germanic Holy Roman Empire] so that you could rule all nations."[9] Against the claims of England and France, it was actually the Germans who were God's chosen people.

These claims of pedigree and destiny were buttressed by the popularized view that the Romans themselves, in the person of the ancient Roman historian Tacitus, long ago admitted the moral superiority of the German tribes to the ancient decadent Romans (the ancestors of the current decadent Romans). Tacitus singled out a Germanic hero, the chieftain Arminius (18 BC–AD 19), as a singular example of the superiority of the Teutonic tribes, a man whose virtues shine in comparison to the depraved first-century AD Roman Caesars such as Tiberius, Caligula, and Nero. These depraved Caesars, to the German propagandists of the early fifteenth century, were the immoral equivalent of the current Roman pontiffs.[10]

Arminius thereby became a kind of resurrected cult hero in Germany. By the beginning of the 1500s, he was seen as the embodiment of German national aspirations against Rome. And there was no greater champion of the nationalist myth of Arminius than the German humanist Ulrich von Hutten, friend of Luther, debunker of the "Donation of Constantine," and author of a book entitled *Arminius*.[11]

In addition, there was a genre of books written in the 1400s—*Gamaleon*, *Reformatio Sigismundi*, and *Book of a Hundred Chapters* being the most important—that prophesied that a German emperor would soon arise, a kind of reforming, messianic priest-king, who would destroy the power of Rome, reform the papacy, and reestablish the Church in Germany—a purer, primitive Church, as God had intended, freed from Roman corruption. We know that Luther read and favorably quoted the *Reformatio Sigismundi*[12] and that for countless Germans a reformed Church meant the establishment of a German national Church.

Nationalism Versus the Pope at the Time of the Reformation

As Michael Wilks observes, "In the course of the fourteenth and fifteenth centuries this equation of *ecclesia* and *terra*, Church and land, spread to most parts of Europe," and thus the splintering of the Catholic Church under nationalist pressure was already well under way *before* the Reformation. "The result," declares Wilks, "was that the Reformation became a virtual inevitability as Europe came to accept this territorial doctrine of the Church as being essentially a collection of 'lands', of independent Israels. And this new— or rather, very old—conception of a church as a territory, as a defined geographical area, was bound to be inherently anti-papal."[13]

It is certainly debatable whether nationalism made the Reformation inevitable (after all, the Catholic Church remained larger than the national Churches that broke away from it), but what is certainly beyond debate is that nationalism greatly exacerbated the religious conflicts of the time, and that it was a major factor in the consequent religious wars of the late 1500s and early 1600s. It also helps explain why these wars ended on the principle of *cuius regio, eius religio*, "whose realm, his religion." Historians have tended to see this as a political result of intractable religious differences, but it may be more accurate to call it a religious result of intractable political differences.

We'll take that question up about the religious wars in a later chapter. But one thing should be very clear from this chapter: nationalism contributed immensely to the division of Christianity in the 1500s, making it far more difficult to bring about reform and almost impossible to retain the unity of Christendom.

How Neo-Pagan Machiavellian Kings Used the Reformation

In the previous chapter on the rise of nationalism and national Churches, we found that prior to the Reformation medieval kings wanted to rule over their own territorial Churches. But this doesn't necessarily mean that they were political connivers who, having no faith of their own, sought to use faith as an instrument of purely political aspirations. In many cases, these kings believed that God had chosen them to rule, like King David, over their domain, and this rule included the care of the Church. We must not assume that they were necessarily being Machiavellian.

Which brings us to the subject of this chapter. We need to uncover another kind of political ruler, one who has his origins in the Renaissance revival of paganism. These kings did not consider themselves heirs of King David. They wanted to return to the pagan world by stripping away Judaism and Christianity, and like the great pagan kings, use religion as an entirely subordinate instrument of political control.

We may call them the Machiavellian Princes, after the most ruthless strategist of this approach, even though they are ultimately rooted in the pagan notion (given to us by Livy, Polybius, and Plutarch, and polished by Averroes) that religions are false yet handy political instruments for the secular rulers. These Machiavellians directly affect the Reformation, both on the Catholic and Protestant side, by their desire to use the Christian divisions to their advantage, both in war and in peace. They are not interested in truth—as true reformers are—but utility, and therefore regard religious quarrelers as useful idiots at best.

Machiavellianism should be distinguished from "Erastianism" (the Protestant doctrine of state supremacy over the Church) and "Caesaropapism" (the largely Byzantine or Eastern Orthodox practice of the emperor directing the Church). While both entail the subordination of Church to state, that subordination could be a good faith effort of a Christian king or emperor to oversee the good order of the churches in his domain. (That doesn't mean it's a good idea, however.) But Machiavellianism is something different. It is the bad faith effort of an irreligious king to use religion to rule the unruly. Yet the Machiavellian has an obvious interest in making common cause with the Erastian or the Caesaropapist in order to weaken the Church so that it can be politically dominated. Given that Machiavelli himself was a master counselor of deceit, it can be difficult to discern sincerely religious rulers from Machiavelli's disciples.

While Niccolò Machiavelli (1469–1527) is perhaps the foremost proponent of ruthless and amoral statecraft (at least up to his time in western Europe), he had at least one important predecessor in Marsilius of Padua (1275–1342) who was equally influential at the time of the Reformation, if not more so. Readers, take note of the dates of Marsilius and Machiavelli. Marsilius lived about two centuries *before* the Reformation. Machiavelli penned his most famous treatise, *The Prince*, about five years *before* Luther penned his *Ninety-Five Theses*, and its influence was felt immediately, penetrating the continent and as far away as the court of King Henry VIII.

That is very important for our understanding of the Reformation and its aftermath. The idea that an unbelieving political ruler should *use* Christianity, subordinating it to his political aims, had significantly influenced political thinking in Europe *before* the Reformation got rolling. The importance of this historical insight cannot be overestimated, because while it is often assumed that religious differences *caused* the political divisions and bloody wars of the Reformation, it is in fact the case that nationalism and Machiavellianism played an enormous role in the fanning of religious differences into wars of nationalist or princely ambition. Indeed, *cuius regio, eius religio* was, from the Machiavellian perspective, the desired outcome, allowing rulers complete control of religion for political purposes.

Marsilius of Padua and the New Averroist Emperor

Marsilius wrote when the Holy Roman Empire was at one of its lowest points, at least in terms of the emperor's power.[1] He was, at this time, very much a tool of the German noble and ecclesiastical electors, and the one way he could try to get out from under their control was through balancing off their power with whatever financial power he could pull from Italy and the Papal States as Rome's protector. The obvious temptation for a hard-pressed emperor was either to make war on the pope, if the pope wasn't sufficiently forthcoming, or to install his own pope (who in turn, by tradition, crowned the emperor).

This imperial temptation was given philosophical justification by Marsilius of Padua in his book *Defensor Pacis* (1234). Marsilius was deeply influenced by the Islamic philosopher, Averroes, who (we recall) believed that philosophers should rule, using religion as an instrument to keep the rabble under control. The great medievalist Étienne Gilson correctly called *Defensor Pacis* "as perfect an example of political Averroism as one could wish for."[2] Following in Averroes' skeptical footsteps, Marsilius subordinated religion to philosophy, and hence the Church to the state. The political goal of Marsilius was simple: to establish imperial control of the papacy, and secular political control of the Church.

Although he lived in a time when outright atheism would certainly be harshly punished, Marsilius let his true beliefs peek through the text at key points. For example, Marsilius wryly noted that, "although some of the [ancient pagan] philosophers who founded…laws or religions did not accept or believe in human resurrection and that life which is called eternal, they nevertheless feigned and persuaded others that it exists and that in it pleasures and pains are in accordance with the qualities of human deeds in this mortal life, in order that they might thereby induce in men reverence and fear of God, and a desire to flee the vices and to cultivate the virtues." The threats and promises of religion were necessary to make the masses behave. Therefore, "these philosophers feigned to be the maker of such laws and the commander of their observance, under the threat of promise of eternal reward for doers of good and punishment for doers of evil." These religious ruses kept the unwashed and unphilosophic multitude under control and therefore benefitted everyone by providing peace. "Hence…the peace or tranquility of states and the sufficient life of men for the status of the present world were preserved with less difficulty; which was the end intended by these wise men laying down such laws or religions."[3]

Marsilius' implied lesson was that, for the sake of peace now, in our own Christian time, clever rulers must follow the wisdom of the ancient pagans. The kinds of arguments that Marsilius made to achieve this goal are extremely important, in light of what would soon happen in the Reformation.

He first (with seeming piety) declared that the Christian God is so mighty and inscrutably beyond our mere human reason that faith is something "we hold…by simple belief apart from reason."[4] In short, he reduced faith to fideism, and he didn't mean this as a compliment, even though he put it forth in faux reverent terms. For the secular-minded Marsilius, asserting that faith is irrational fideism—something that "must be piously held"—was to reaffirm the pagan view (found in Livy, Polybius, and Plutarch, and affirmed in Averroes) that religion was entirely non-rational bunk, but useful bunk nonetheless.

To assure its utility to the secular ruler, Marsilius asserted (almost two centuries before Luther) a doctrine of *sola scriptura*, arguing that the faith is grounded in "Scripture alone." The goal of this rooting of the faith entirely in Scripture was not genuinely pious but deviously tactical: it was meant to undermine the authority of the pope and therefore of the universal Church.[5] For the sake of peace and good government, Marsilius believed the Holy Roman Emperor should appoint all priests and bishops (including the bishop of Rome) and control, through his own political-secular council, the interpretation of Scripture.[6]

Marsilius even supports his argument through selective interpretation of the Bible, leaning heavily on those passages of Holy Writ that imply complete obedience of Christians (the pope most decidedly not excepted) to Caesar.[7] So, we are told by Marsilius, Jesus Christ *himself* demanded complete subservience to "human laws, and he commanded every human soul to observe these and to obey the men who ruled in accordance with them, at least the commands which were not opposed to the law of eternal salvation."[8] Given that the political imperium was, for Marsilius, to be in control of the interpretation of Scripture, it's hard to imagine a situation arising where the political ruler would judge his own laws to be "opposed to the law of eternal salvation."

Marsilius thereby handed the Holy Roman Emperor the keys to the Church, making the pope, Church appointees, and Holy Scripture itself into political instruments. Citing appropriate Gospel passages,[9] Marsilius implied that the emperor should reduce the Church to apostolic poverty (and thus enlarge the imperial treasury). Stripping riches from the Church, he asserted, would be of the greatest benefit to Christianity.

> For they who are teachers or pastors of others, and who possess such riches, do more to destroy men's faith and devotion by their contrary deeds and examples than they do to strengthen them by their words.... For if the future

just judgment of God in the world to come is indeed believed in by most of the Roman pontiffs and their cardinals and the other priests or bishops...then by what conscience in accordance with God—let them answer, I beg—do they seize or steal, at every opportunity, all the temporal goods they can, which devout believers have bequeathed for the sustenance of gospel ministers and other poor persons, and donate or bequeath them to their relatives, or to any other persons not in need, obviously despoiling the poor thereby? And again—let them answer, I beg—by what conscience in accordance with the Christian religion do they consume the goods of the poor on so many unnecessary things—horses, estates, banquets, and other vanities and pleasures, open and concealed—when according to the Apostle in the first epistle to Timothy, last chapter, they ought to be content with food and shelter for ministering the gospel.[10]

This passage of righteous indignation could have come right out of the mouth, or pen, of Martin Luther, or any of a number of Protestant reformers (or sincere Catholic reformers, for that matter). It points directly to real abuses among the Church hierarchy. The difference is that Marsilius' indignation isn't actually righteous. As an Averroist, he was seeking to subordinate Christianity to a this-worldly politics, just as the ancient pagans had done, and he wasn't afraid to use true Christian righteous indignation to further his ends.

The practical implications of this argument were not lost on Pope John XXII, enthroned as he was, amidst the luxuries of the

Avignon papacy. Nor were they lost on the enemy of John, the would-be emperor, Ludwig of Bavaria, who simultaneously wanted to dominate Italy and have a pope anoint him as actual emperor.

While Pope John XXII was not amused by the *Defensor Pacis* and declared Marsilius heretical on multiple counts, Ludwig of Bavaria was so amused that he made Marsilius his court "theologian" and political advisor. Ludwig then marched into Rome (with Marsilius as his Imperial Vicar), and deposed the absent Pope John and put his own compliant man, Nicholas V, on the throne of St. Peter in April 1328.

On top of this immediate practical effect of Marsilius' teaching, his arguments were extremely influential across Europe, and directly or indirectly on Luther who cited the same passages as Marsilius about the necessity of the Church obeying Caesar. That doesn't mean Luther was a disciple of Marsilius, but that Luther unwittingly supported those who were.

The Infamous Machiavelli

Machiavelli was a man, like Marsilius, who read the ancient pagan philosophers very carefully, and concluded that pagan wisdom was superior to Christian wisdom, and therefore that Christianity was a large, long-lasting historical mistake. He did not advocate doing away with Christianity. Rather, it should be treated like the ancient pagan philosophers treated the religions of their time, as just one more irrational superstition that could be made into a political instrument. While it's not clear that he was influenced by Marsilius, Machiavelli was certainly influenced by the same pagan historians.

In Machiavelli's *Discourses on Livy* he taught a now-familiar lesson, using the ancient historians Livy, Polybius, and Plutarch. The great philosopher kings Romulus, Numa, and Tullus, he tells the reader, all "turned to religion as a thing altogether necessary... to maintain a civilization." The masses of men cannot be ruled by reason, nor can they be controlled simply by the brute force of the ruler. The cure for this problem: "wise men who wish to take away this difficulty have recourse to God."[11]

Like the ancient philosophers, the great atheist Machiavelli did not want unbelief to be trumpeted to the very masses whom religion was being used to control. Rejection of Christianity, atheism, was only for the elite, for the ruling princes. Rulers will still need religion to rule, and Christianity was the religion at hand. That's why Machiavelli, the atheist, could say in all earnestness that "Those princes or those republics that wish to maintain themselves...have above everything else to maintain the ceremonies of their religion uncorrupt and hold them always in veneration; for one can have no greater indication of the ruin of a province than to see the divine cult disdained." And so, "All things that arise in favor of that religion they should favor and magnify, even though they judge them false...."[12]

A ruler therefore needs to be "a great pretender and dissembler," so that "he should appear all mercy, all faith, all honesty, all humanity, all religion," and "nothing is more necessary to appear to have than this last quality." Religious appearance is one thing, done for the sake of upholding the fiction of belief. But a truly wise prince, "since he is often under a necessity, to maintain his state," finds that he must sometimes act "against faith, against charity, against humanity, against religion." For this reason, and against his show of public piety, he must "know how to enter into evil, when forced by necessity."[13]

That brings us to a second part of Machiavelli's thought, one for which he is equally famous. In Machiavelli's most renowned work, *The Prince*, he lays out the lessons for a ruler who is able to shake loose the bonds of Christianity that limit his actions—the belief in God, personal immortality, heaven and hell—so that he can engage in ruthless and remorseless *realpolitik* statecraft. A prince under the spell of Christianity necessarily desires to be good, but that's precisely what makes good Christians bad princes. "For a man who wants to make a profession of good in all regards must come to ruin among so many who are not good. Hence it is necessary to a prince, if he wants to maintain himself, to learn to be able not to be good, and to use this and not use it according to necessity."[14]

We can now see the two parts of Machiavelli come together, especially what he contributes to the already existing stream of Averroism. The ruthless Machiavellian prince cannot be ruthless unless he sheds his own Christian belief. He must have no pangs of conscience when, for the sake of political survival or gain, he has to do some evil act forbidden by Christian morality, an act that would land him in hell. Happily, he doesn't believe in hell, but this same Machiavellian prince must pretend to be all piety publicly, because he needs Christianity as a very useful tool for controlling his state.

For Machiavelli, Pope Alexander VI was a stellar example of the union of pagan wisdom and ruthless *realpolitik*, which speaks sad volumes for the state of the Catholic Church just before the time of Luther; but it also highlights how Protestant attacks on papal corruption could vindicate a cynical, Machiavellian assessment of Christianity, and how Protestantism could thus be used by Machiavellian princes (especially those inspired by reformers, like Luther, who emphasized biblical passages counseling obedience to princes).

The Machiavellian Reformation of Henry VIII

While Pope Alexander was a perfect example of Machiavelli's cynicism toward religion, England's Henry VIII provided an exemplar of a Machiavellian king, ruthlessly subordinating the Church to the crown. To understand this claim, we need to step back a bit from Henry's time, and look at the situation in England about two centuries before the Reformation.

No Church is more rooted in nationalism than the Anglican Church—and for very good historical reasons. As noted previously, from at least the time of the Hundred Years' War, the English had seen themselves as a chosen people with King Edward III (1327–1377) likening himself to King David. In historian J. W. McKenna's words, "Edward III, who claimed the French crown itself, intensified a rivalry with the French kings over the mystical attributes of regality. In so doing he laid the foundation for a distinctively English political theology which could support and underlay both Henrician assertions of autonomous national sovereignty and Elizabethan assurances of Britannic godliness."[15] McKenna continues, this "ideology of mystical kingship," purloined from the French, "underlies the first great age of vernacular English political and literary patriotism and the new language of nascent English nationalism,"[16] which included (we might be surprised to find out) the effort to translate the Bible into English.

One of the great English reformers, and translators of the Bible, was John Wycliffe (1320–1384), often called the "morning star" of the Reformation. But while Wycliffe was a passionate reformer, in the political context of his time he was also a servant of the crown's ambition. As historian Michael Wilks puts it, "what Edward III needed was a justification of his right to act as a supreme ecclesiastical overlord on a Biblical basis," a right that would be significantly enhanced by a translation of Scripture into English, which would create "the Bible as specifically the book of the *ecclesia Anglicana*...and that was what Wycliffe gave him."[17]

Pope Gregory XI condemned Wycliffe as a follower of Marsilius of Padua.[18] He wasn't, but Wycliffe's call for political control of the clergy, the rejection of the papacy, and the disendowment of the Church could certainly sound that way. To Wycliffe, however, these were reforms that would restore England's original, unspoiled, apostolic Church. In Edith Tatnall's estimation, "Wycliffe had an idea of a kind of primitive state of innocence and virtue in the English Church, to which the temporal lords could return it by taking from it the large accretions of temporal property that had caused its fall."[19]

Indeed, Wycliffe believed the king had a *moral obligation* to return the English Church to its primitive purity.[20] But Wycliffe's theology could easily be used by a king seeking his own monetary benefit, and it was, almost two centuries later, by the cynical, Marsilian circle around Henry VIII for different, Machiavellian ends than Wycliffe had imagined.[21] It is no coincidence that one of King Henry's chief henchmen, Thomas Cromwell, subsidized the English translation of Marsilius' *Defensor Pacis*.[22]

And Marsilius was not the only influence on the Henrician circle. We also know that not only had the English humanist Lord Morley (circa 1480–1556) directed Cromwell to take up the wisdom of Machiavelli,[23] but that Cardinal Reginald Pole (1500–1558) believed Cromwell had sold his soul to Machiavelli (and that Machiavelli had sold his to the devil himself).[24]

So we should not be surprised by Henry VIII being one of history's most notorious tyrants, England's Nero, as some have put it, snatching up as much lucre as he could from the suppression and forced dissolution of English monasteries, savagely destroying his political and theological opponents (as evidenced in his brutality against the Pilgrimage of Grace, undertaken by those who questioned his break with Rome and his emptying of the monasteries into his pockets), and callously dispensing with his wives, all the while claiming to be the holy head of the English Church.[25] Henry VIII's reformation of the English Church had little to do with the religious goals of the Reformers (Henry had actually been an early critic of Luther) and everything to do with Henry wanting to divorce one woman and marry another (and another, and another, and so on). But above all, his goal was absolute political power, and that entailed asserting royal supremacy over the Church, a Marsilian goal gotten by Machiavellian means.

But Henry was not an exception. His ambition to subordinate Church to state was shared by rulers across Europe. Luther's revolt and its aftermath offered them an opportunity; and in no place were rulers' motives more mixed, because of power being so dispersed, than in Luther's Germany, the very cradle of the Reformation.[26]

CHAPTER NINE

YES, LUTHER REALLY WAS A VERY FLAWED MAN

We come, at long last, to our consideration of Martin Luther, the central figure of the Reformation. Just as Catholics need to take a deep, hard, honest look at the actual corruption of the papacy rather than pretend that all popes have been saints, so also Protestants need to take a deep, hard, honest look at Martin Luther rather than pretend that *he* was a saint. We're not out to tar him as a heretic or the moral equivalent of Pope Alexander VI. That would be entirely unfair. But honesty demands that we look at Luther closely, and describe him warts and all.[1]

I hope we've made it clear that Martin Luther did not act alone. The cries for reform dinned the air throughout Europe, and flooded the presses as well, and would have done so had Hans and Margarethe never had their famous son. (On an interesting note, his parents were Hans and Margarethe *Luder*, not Luther. Martin later added first an "h" and then, dropping the "d," a "t" later on.) But there is no denying that he was central in ensuring that these cries for reformation became the Reformation. Understanding the centrality of Luther demands that we take an honest, sober look at the man and the movement.

How the Man Became a Monk

There are a few big "what ifs" in Luther's life. To begin with, he hadn't meant to be a monk, but to go into the law. His father, Hans, was the son of a peasant farmer who'd made good as a miner, then leased his own copper pit, and thereby became rather prosperous. Pushing Martin up the social ladder, he sent his son to the University of Erfurt for a bachelor's degree, then a master's degree, and finally on to law school.

We might well then ask, "what if" Luther had become a lawyer? Would there have been a Reformation? Perhaps not. But again, there would have been a reformation, since there was already one working its way around Europe, and had been for some time.

What form that reformation would have taken we'll never know, because of what happened in the summer of 1505. To put this event in context, we must recall the larger atmosphere of dread and drama noted in previous chapters. Many thought that they were living in the end times, and that God in his anger at Church corruption was gathering the storms of the apocalypse to chastise Europe for its sins, the very sins that cried to heaven for a deep reform of the Church and Christian life.

As we've seen, one great sign of God's displeasure was the ceaseless press of Islam on Christian Europe. Just as God had brought the pagan Assyrians and Babylonians to chastise Israel, so also He was bringing an alien Muslim horde to punish Christendom for its failure to reform. Another sign was the Black Plague, which far from disappearing with the fourteenth century, kept lashing Europe as a seeming scourge. It was once again moving through Germany that very summer of 1505. In 1527, 1535, and 1539 it would hit Wittenberg, the city Luther would soon make famous, and two of his brothers would succumb to the plague.

Human history and nature both seemed to be speaking God's wrath against the corruptions of Christianity and society itself. On July 2, 1505, nature seemed to speak very directly to Martin Luther on his trip back to Erfurt from visiting his parents. Caught in a violent storm, he was knocked to the ground by an earthshattering thunderclap. In his own retrospective words, "Suddenly surrounded by the terror and agony of death, I felt constrained to make a vow." And so he cried out, "Help me, St. Anne; I will become a monk!"[2]

An understandable reaction, but it was a vow that he both kept and deeply regretted. On top of that, Martin's integrity in keeping that vow, and entering the Order of the Hermits of St. Augustine located in Erfurt on July 17, 1505, made his father, Hans, absolutely furious.

Considered on its own, and in the context of Luther's time, this seemingly sudden vow made sense. Monasticism was understood to be a far more serious affirmation of Christianity, a step up from life in this world and toward the next in answering Christ's call to follow him and give up all one's goods and even one's family. So Jesus told the rich young man, "If you want to be perfect, go, sell your possessions and give to the poor, and you will have treasure in heaven. Then come, follow me" (Mt 19:21). To which he adds, "And everyone who has left houses or brothers or sisters or father or mother or wife or children or fields for my sake will receive a hundred times as much and will inherit eternal life" (Mt 19:29).

Or perhaps even more appropriate to the apocalyptic atmosphere of Luther's time were the words of the celibate St. Paul, spoken by him in the belief that his were the end times ushering in the return of Christ, "I wish that all of you were as I am. But each of you has your own gift from God; one has this gift, another has that. Now to the unmarried and the widows I say: It is good for them to stay unmarried, as I do. But if they cannot control themselves, they should marry, for it is better to marry than to burn with passion" (I Cor 7:7–9). The vocation to celibate service to God was thereby considered a gift, one taken up in imitation of St. Paul himself.

In the Catholic context of the time, then, it's less surprising that Luther would make such a vow. The calls for reform were calls to renewed holiness. So, it's not a stretch—if we enter Luther's mind at this decisive moment—that he sincerely thought becoming a monk was the kind of holy seriousness which the dark and punishing clouds of the sky, echoing the hammering of Islam and the plague, seemed to be calling for.

Luther answered that call, much to his immediate and subsequent regret. Luther did not want to be a monk.

Just for the reader's information, I know of no religious order that would, today, allow someone to enter under such conditions. Today, applicants to religious life are first given extensive interviews, and then, if provisionally accepted, are put through a series of formative steps that test the seriousness of their call, before being allowed to take formal and permanent vows. You can't just hop into a monastery, and that's a good reform.

I say this not just to assure readers that the Catholic Church has (thankfully) reformed its mode of acceptance into religious life, but also to bring up another "what if." What if the Order of the Hermits of St. Augustine had responded with prudent and pastoral skepticism to Luther's rash vow? Or failing that, put him through a three-year program of discernment *before* allowing him to take a formal vow? We can be fairly certain that he would have become a lawyer married to a plump, loving but rather dictatorial German wife. He may still have been a great reformer—and he did in fact end up marrying a plump, loving, but rather dictatorial ex-nun of a German wife—but he would not have undertaken reform through a wrenching, personal repudiation of a religious vocation that he did not, in fact, have. We'll presently see what a difference that might have made.

Discovering the Seeds of Salvation by Faith Alone

But Luther did in fact try to become a good monk. We note previously that, as an obedient monk, he went to Rome on behalf of his Augustinian religious order in the winter of 1510–1511, and was scandalized by witnessing, up close and ugly, the corruption seething under the unwatchful eye of Pope Julius II—flagrant blasphemy, mockery of the saints, and a priest joking about the Holy Eucharist.[3]

In 1512, he became a doctor of theology, and, in turn, a professor of biblical theology at Wittenberg University in Saxony (recently founded by the Elector of Saxony, Frederick the Wise, soon to be Luther's protector).

Being a professor of biblical theology allowed him to focus intensely on Holy Writ, lecturing on St. Paul's Letter to the Romans from the spring of 1515 to the fall of 1516. This close study, in the context of his own wrestling with a vocation he did not have, was decisive, as he later made clear in retrospect. "I hated that word 'righteousness of God,'" he confessed. "Though I lived as a monk without reproach, I felt that I was a sinner before God with an extremely disturbed conscience. I could not believe that he was placated by my satisfaction." But St. Paul provided an escape:

> At last, by the mercy of God, meditating day and night, I gave heed to the context of the words, namely, "in it the righteousness of God is revealed," as it is written, "He who through faith is righteous shall live." There I began to understand that the righteousness of God is that by which the righteous lives by a gift of God, namely by faith….Here I felt that I was altogether born again and had entered paradise itself through open gates. There a totally other face of the entire Scripture showed itself to me."[4]

All his toilsome efforts at fulfilling the demands of his vocation, all his attempts at becoming a good and holy monk, were thereby seen in a new light: as a very unpleasant but effective providential lesson that salvation was a free gift, one given in response to faith, a gift that God offers through the sacrifice of Jesus Christ, not something that one earns by his own actions.

From this angle, his vow to become a monk began to appear not only rash but—even worse—an attempt to *earn* salvation through his own efforts, through his own "works." To Luther, monasticism soon seemed scandalous; the idea that monastic works were of any use to salvation was a mockery of Christ's own offering of himself on the cross. If we were "justified" (made just, made holy, made righteous) by our own efforts, then what did we need Christ for? Salvation, for Luther, surely came from faith alone, (*sola fide*), not by works. Centuries upon centuries of Catholic error, he thought, had obscured this central Christian truth. In fact, that error was an ancient heresy, Pelagianism, the belief that our individual efforts could win our salvation.

From the Catholic angle, by contrast, it appeared that Luther had constructed his understanding of theology to escape from the misery of his hastily taken vow. His doctrine of justification by faith alone meant that the whole monastic enterprise was ill-conceived, which conveniently allowed him to break that vow, and reenter the world, where his true vocation lay. If he had stayed a layman, then no such crisis of faith would have affected him. There were plenty of men and women in religious life who found deep fulfillment with the walls of a monastery or convent.

Thus, to Catholics of the time, Luther's situation was not one of genuine religious insight, but parallel to someone caught in a bad marriage who destroys the institution of marriage in order to escape from his own unpleasant bind. Further, from the Catholic point of view, Luther was falling into the heresy of antinomianism, which affirms such a strong doctrine of grace, that all human efforts at becoming good are entirely indifferent. If that's the case, some argued, then why not live it up, if nothing you do, one way or another, contributes to your own salvation? In fact, some of Luther's followers did, to his chagrin, become antinomians. Finally, as an offshoot of this strong doctrine of grace, and in line with antinomianism, it was soon asserted (most forcefully by John Calvin, and against Luther) that since there was nothing we could contribute to our own salvation, it all rests on God's inscrutable will. The eternal God must then have willed who would be saved and who damned, even before he created the world—the so-named doctrine of Double Predestination. If such were the case, Catholics thought, why bother doing anything?

The Infamous Indulgences

Coming back to Luther himself, it was the abuse of the sale of indulgences—essentially, buying your way out of the necessary penance to make amends for sin—that brought Luther's hatred for Church corruption and his critique of Catholic thinking together. In October 1517 Luther issued his *Disputation on the Power and Efficacy of Indulgences* (or the *Ninety-Five Theses*, as it's more popularly called). According to legend, he nailed it onto the door of the Castle Church at Wittenberg on October 31, 1517. Many academics, however, now think he mailed it to his archbishop, Albrecht of Brandenburg.[5] In these famous *Theses*, Luther called for a disputation, not a revolution. A disputation is a formal, serious discussion, and his aim in calling for one was the correction of abuses, not rejection of indulgences. Moreover, he wrote it not in defiance of the papacy, but with especial deference to Pope Leo X, the Medici pope.

Thus, we find in thesis ninety-one, "If...indulgences were preached in accordance with the spirit and mind of the pope, all these difficulties [mentioned among the previous ninety theses] would be easily overcome, and, indeed, cease to exist."[6] The focus was on reform,[7] as thesis sixty-nine makes clear: "Bishops and curates...must receive the commissaries of the papal indulgences with all reverence.... But they are under a much greater obligation to watch closely and attend carefully lest these men preach their own fancies instead of what the pope commissioned." Thesis seventy-one even says "Let him be anathema and accursed who denies the apostolic character of the indulgences," but seventy-two warns, "let him be blessed who is on his guard against the wantonness of license of the pardon-merchants' words."

Luther's protest was occasioned by a now infamous Dominican friar named Johann Tetzel who was selling indulgences in the summer of 1517 just outside of Saxony where Luther resided. Unfortunately, the archbishop to whom Luther protested was himself an example of the Church corruption that needed to be reformed. Albrecht of Brandenburg was, in the words of historian Diarmaid MacCulloch, not a holy man but "an extreme example of the European noblemen who regarded the Church as an asset to be exploited for their family, in his case the great German dynasty of the Hohenzollern. He was determined to use his very considerable talents to continue the Hohenzollerns' steady accumulation of power."[8]

Albrecht bought himself the electoral archbishopric of Mainz. That set him up nicely, both in terms of power (as an Elector of the

Holy Roman Emperor) and eventually money (in an archbishopric sure to yield a high return on his original investment). But in the short term, he was saddled him with a wealth of debt and the necessity of the pope's dispensation (Albrecht was technically too young to be an archbishop). So Albrecht cut a deal with Pope Leo X: a papal dispensation was his if he would allow the selling of indulgences within his territory, the money to be divided evenly between archbishop and pope (who was trying to pay for the remodeling of St. Peter's Basilica). Thus did one corruption (the sale of Church offices) feed another (the sale of indulgences).

But if the Archbishop was corrupt and uninterested in Luther's *Ninety-Five Theses*, the printing press forced him to change his mind, as this seemingly arcane academic document suddenly appeared all over Germany, printed in both Latin and German so that every literate person could read it; and this put Luther's protest into an entirely different context—not just one to be debated among clerics, but one that touched on popular discontent and German national ambitions we've mentioned previously.

Given the new speed of printing, Luther's complaints could not be ignored, and he was summoned to Augsburg in 1518, where Cardinal Thomas Cajetan (a reformer) tried but failed to get Luther to recant, and Luther, fearing that he would be kidnapped, fled. Other papal emissaries attempted to convince Luther he was wrong until Pope Leo X finally decided the renegade monk was incorrigible and excommunicated him in 1521 after Luther publicly burned the papal bull *Exsurge Domine*, which set out the Pope's objections to Luther's theology. Luther was then summoned before the imperial Diet (congress) at Worms in 1521. The Holy Roman Emperor Charles V saw theological dissent as a threat to the universal Church and thus to the peace of the Empire. Luther was humble enough under examination, confessing that he might have been a little hot-headed and that as a sinner he may have gone too far in his public statements following the release of his *Ninety-Five Theses*.

Some of these statements were a bit steamy, to say the very least. Luther had written that there was "no remedy" for reforming the papacy "but with the sword," so that, "we" (lay rulers and reformers alike) must "fling ourselves with all our weapons upon these masters of perdition, these cardinals, these popes, and all this sink of Roman sodomy that ceaselessly corrupts the church of God and wash our hands in their blood so that we may free ourselves and all who belong to us from this most dangerous fire...."[9]

At the Diet, he curbed his flaming rhetoric. He was even willing to admit error *if* he could be corrected by the truth as found in Scripture (not canon law, a papal bull, or a statement by a Church council). In his words (which are the source of the famous fictionalized "Here I stand" speech),

> Unless I am convicted by scripture and by plain reason (I do not believe in the authority of either popes or councils by themselves, for it is plain that they have often erred and contradicted each other) in those scriptures that I have presented, for my conscience is captive to the Word of God, I cannot and I will not recant anything, for to go against conscience is neither right nor safe. God help me, Amen.[10]

Emperor Charles V was not impressed. Luther's hot rhetoric was plainly seditious, and heretics citing Scripture was an old and dangerous problem. In May 1521, the emperor issued the imperial Edict of Worms, declaring Luther a heretic, even while allowing him safe passage out of town.

Condemned by pope and emperor, Luther won the support of German princes. Whatever their theological leanings, it is clear they had an interest in using Lutheranism to assert their independence, part of which entailed the creation of a German Church, or Churches, since each would be subordinate to a respective principality. For Luther, these rulers—not the pope or the emperor—were the ones to whom true Christians owed their obedience (as per Scriptural passages affirming civil authority). He had put this in writing in his tract *An Appeal to the Ruling Class of German Nationality as to the Amelioration of the State of Christendom* (1520).

In his *Appeal*, Luther continually referred to those defending the papacy as "Romanists," a title pitting Germans versus Italians in a nationalist battle. Luther informed his readers that the Romanist Church was controlled by Satan, that the pope was the Antichrist, and since the Church's "princes of hell" were not going to allow reform, the German lay princes would have to reform the Church instead.[11]

Luther argued that the "Romanists" were shielded by three walls that had to be torn down: one, that the sacred power is superior to the secular power; two, that no one but the pope can expound Scripture; and three, that only a pope can summon a Church council.[12]

To batter down these walls, Luther first declared that baptism makes us all priests, therefore a king or emperor through baptism "has already been consecrated priest, bishop, or pope...."[13] This is the so-called doctrine of the "priesthood of all believers," which immediately leveled the playing field between the spiritual and temporal powers, popes, and princes. Why should a prince, who was now a pope, obey a pope who was merely acting like a prince?

As to the second wall, since princes are all priests and popes, no one has a monopoly on the interpretation of Scripture. So, declared Luther boldly, "why then should we not be entitled to taste or test, and to judge what is right or wrong in the faith?"[14] Not the pope, not tradition, not the Church, nor any council, but Holy Scripture itself was the sole, infallible source of authority for the Christian (hence the later Reformation battle cry, *sola scriptura*). He now put that authority of interpretation into the hands of every believer, who could use it against the pope (or, as it turned out, against each other).

The third wall, Luther stated triumphantly, "falls without more ado when the first two are demolished," because a lay ruler is as much a pope as a pope, and in that capacity, he can call a reform council. It was, after all, the Emperor Constantine, Luther points out, who called the Council of Nicaea.[15]

With the battering of these three walls, the Reformation truly got under way, but with some consequences that Luther did not foresee.

Multiplying Reformers and Luther's Headaches

After the Diet of Worms, as a declared heretic, Luther had to go into hiding, holing up at Wartburg Castle near Eisenach under the protection of the German Elector, Frederick the Wise. As an Elector of Holy Roman Emperors, there was a limit to how far he could be pushed around by Catholic emperor Charles V. But that didn't mean it was safe for Luther to wander about either, so he spent 1521 thinking and writing.

This relative peace was soon broken by events back in Wittenberg. There, reformers inspired directly by Luther, began taking his doctrinal principles—*sola scriptura*, the priesthood of all believers, and justification by faith alone—to places Luther himself thought were heretical.

This marked the beginning of the essential doctrinal splits among Protestants, and since it happened so quickly—in less than five years from Luther's publication of the *Ninety-Five Theses*—it convinced the papacy, but even more important, those who passionately desired reform from *within* the Catholic Church, that Luther's way led to disintegration rather than reform.

Luther himself was immensely distressed, and we can see why. A radical reformer similar to himself, Andreas von Karlstadt, and a group called the "Zwickau prophets" had alighted in Wittenberg in 1521. Basing their arguments upon Luther's notion of justification by faith alone, they rejected all the sacraments—and claimed that there was no support in Scripture for infant baptism, and perhaps not even for adult baptism. Furthermore, some of their followers rejected the doctrine of original sin, the notion that marriage was permanent (it was not, after all, a sacrament), and argued in favor of polygamy (such as existed in the Old Testament).

Even more infuriating for Luther, who still believed in the necessity of baptism and the reality of the Eucharist, was that these reformers were attacking the Mass as an idolatrous act and were smashing up church statues, crucifixes, and paintings (even of

Christ himself) as idolatrous. And some transformed the religious idea of the equality of all believers into a political cry for equality and political rebellion.[16]

Luther returned to Wittenberg in March 1522 to condemn these rival reformers. As Diarmaid MacCulloch notes, "He had now seen the effect of letting the idea of Gospel freedom have its head without careful direction. He must now concentrate on creating a shape for what...looked more and more like the structure of a [new] Church."[17] Luther referred to the radicals infesting Wittenberg as the *Schwärmer*, the fanatics, and declared them all to be satanic,[18] and asked the Elector Frederick to expel the reforming rebels from Saxony.

Speaking of Andreas von Karlstadt, Luther complained that he "has deserted us, and...become our worst enemy" because he "seeks to destroy it [the gospel] with cunning interpretation of Scripture."[19]

But these "fanatics," as Luther called them, were actually intelligent scholars of the Bible, or at least some of them were. Karlstadt, for instance, had a doctorate in theology, and as chancellor of Wittenberg University had actually awarded Luther *his* doctorate. And some of these fanatics would go on to build significant branches of the Protestant Reformation.

Huldrych Zwingli in Zürich, Switzerland, for one, shared Luther's beginning points, but rejected baptism and the Eucharist as sacraments, decided that all religious images were idolatrous, banned music in church, and dismissed the idea of fasting during Lent (fasting was a "work" and unnecessary since one was saved by faith alone).[20] Zwingli considered himself not a fanatic, but a reformer of Luther's reform.

But even reformers of reform were unsettled by other reformers. "There were...serpents in Zwingli's garden" at Zürich, notes Mac-Culloch wryly, "not angry supporters of the Pope or troublesome Lutherans, but his own most fervent admirers," who were even more Zwinglian Zwinglians. They "read their Bibles as he told them to do...and then drew their own conclusions."[21] That spelled trouble, which is much easier than spelling Huldrych Zwingli.

Whereas Zwingli tried to stay in the good graces of Zürich's town council, his radical followers decided that since baptism was not a sacrament, and there were no infant baptisms in the Bible, then only adults should be baptized—not sacramentally but only as a symbol. So they set about baptizing each other, and then celebrating a non-sacramental communal meal of bread and wine that were only symbols of Christ's body and blood.

For the rebaptizing aspect, they got tagged "Anabaptists," "rebaptizers." The city council, with Zwingli's approval, had them driven out (in fact, four of them were drowned as a symbolic punishment for rebaptizing).[22] It was this Anabaptist branch—which traveled all over the doctrinal map[23]—who were the main radicals of the Reformation.

Other radicals were convinced that, since all images were idolatrous, they ought to be physically destroyed, even humiliated.[24] Thus, an outbreak of iconoclasm began about 1524, not just in Switzerland, but soon spreading to other areas in Northern Europe as well. Images of St. Francis were a favorite target; so were images of the Virgin Mary whose virginity came into dispute. In one case a cathedral's wooden statue of Mary was denounced as a witch and cast in a river. The fact that the wood floated allegedly proved it *was* a witch, so the statue was retrieved and burned.[25]

The Protestant smashing spree of religious art only gained momentum with the arrival of John Calvin (1509–1564), who likewise rejected images based upon his reading of the Old Testament.[26] (Calvin's followers were often called Calvinists, as mentioned above, but their preferred name was the Reformed, capital "R"). A particularly notorious outbreak of iconoclasm was directed at Catholic churches in the Netherlands in 1566 in the wake of Reformed sermons against idolatry.

To Catholics at the time, such iconoclasm was violently irreligious. The educated among them knew that iconoclasm had already been declared heretical in the eighth century, and they no doubt associated iconoclasm with Islam, because the anti-iconic Muslims likewise entered Christian churches and smashed images. For Catholics, Protestantism was heretical and lawless; the apparent lawlessness was all around them after Luther's revolt.

The Peasant Rebellion, Luther's Nightmare

The most shocking bit of lawlessness was the Peasant Rebellion of 1524 to 1525. It took its inspiration directly from Luther's bold defiance of ecclesiastical and imperial authority, and from his principles of *sola scriptura* and every man his own priest. These were not "peasants" as we might think of them, but tenant farmers. Their leaders were the wealthy rural elite and they wanted relief from the burdens imposed on them by landlords, many of which were rich monasteries, churches, and cathedrals.[27]

The rebellion spread quickly all over Europe, and became ever more destructive of life and property. In response, as blame fell heavily upon him, Luther stridently preached obedience to Caesar and the necessity of crushing the rebellion. His famous tract *Against the Robbing and Murdering Gangs of Peasants* issued a clarion call for "anyone who can" to "smash, strangle, and stab, secretly or openly"[28] the rebellious peasants, without fear of conscience, as it was a matter of Christian duty. In a second tract, tartly titled *An Epistle on the Hard Little Book against the Peasants*, Luther argued that princes should kill both the guilty and the innocent indiscriminately until the rebellion ceased.

While this endeared Luther to some of the rulers, it turned many of the ruled against him. Luther was unfazed, declaring later, "All their blood is on my neck. But I know it from our Lord God that he commanded me to speak."[29]And he made his case against the peasants from Scripture, most especially from St. Paul's Letter to the Romans. "Let everyone be subject to the governing authorities, for there is no authority except that which God has established. The authorities that exist have been established by God. Consequently, whoever rebels against the authority is rebelling against what God has instituted, and those who do so will bring judgment on themselves." To make sure the lesson stuck, Luther reminded the peasants of St. Paul's warning about their rulers, "They are God's servants, agents of wrath to bring punishment on the wrongdoer" (Rom 13:1–4).

The Prince in Control of the Lutheran Church

The German princes didn't like disorderly peasants, but they did like Luther's invocations of obedience to secular authority. Richard Marius notes:

> Princes found advantages to going over to the Lutheran side, and for once they read Luther aright when they

pondered his demand for obedience among the people. Luther's stress on obedience became a monotonous theme in his preaching ever afterward. It is far too simple to explain these conversions [of princes] by any one influence. But at least it could be said that these transformations would not have happened had the princes not had proof that Luther supported their right to authority no matter how cruel their authority might be. He could rage against the sins of the nobles; they were content to ignore him since he had proven that his way was finally resignation rather than rebellion.[30]

Luther not only preached obedience in general, but he subordinated the Church to the state and handed over to the princes the power to enforce doctrine, citing the precedent of Emperor Constantine deciding between Arians and Catholics at the Council of Nicaea.[31] Despite his own intentions and the reality of the precedent, Luther was creating the perfect situation for rulers who were disciples of Marsilius or Machiavelli, and who therefore saw his doctrines as politically convenient rather than true.

Historian W. D. J. Cargill Thompson notes another connection to an essential theological aspect in Luther's political thinking: "An inevitable consequence of Luther's rejection of good works as a necessary factor to salvation was that he no longer saw this world as being preparatory to the next, in the sense that what one does in this world contributes directly to one's fate in the next."[32] Thus the kingdom of man was entirely secularized and disconnected from the kingdom of God, and that likewise made way for the new, entirely secular princes, schooled directly or indirectly by Marsilius and Machiavelli.

Giving so much to the secular prince was a problem for Luther, even in his own day. A very great embarrassment in his life, in this regard, was the debacle with greatest prince-protector of the Protestant cause, Landgrave Philip of Hesse. Philip was one of the early princes to declare himself for the Protestant cause. Doing so meant that Luther counted on him for protection and support. That put Luther in a particularly sticky situation when Philip came to him, wanting him to support his desire to marry another wife without unmarrying his first; in other words, Philip wanted divine sanction for bigamy. Philip was a rather notorious philanderer, and suffered from syphilis, so his moral credentials were a bit rusty. Luther and fellow reformer Philip Melanchthon rooted through Scripture to provide the sanction Philip wanted, but begged Philip to keep his second wife and their divine permission slip both a secret, since if it got out, Luther's image would be severely tarnished. That is exactly what happened when the news spread all over Europe, giving Luther's enemies the satisfaction of saying "That's what happens with the doctrine of *sola scriptura* and justification by faith alone—you can get Scripture to let you do *anything*, especially if you're Luther's prince."[33]

We may not be able to sort out what these German princes actually believed, but as the secularizing political philosophies of Marsilius and Machiavelli spread over Europe during the rest of the 1500s and into the 1600s, the ambiguity would only become more acute.

CHAPTER TEN

The Invention of the Printing Press Was a Blessing (and a Curse) for the Reformation

The invention of the printing press separates the Reformation from previous history, and without it, Luther's handwritten *Ninety-Five Theses* would likely have remained on a dusty corner of Archbishop Albrecht of Brandenburg's desk—and Luther would likely have remained a very unhappy monk.[1]

The printing press seems, then, a cause for celebration from the perspective of Protestants, promoting the central Reformation doctrines to a mass audience and printing more Bibles than had existed in all of Christian history before the 1500s. And so it is usually heralded in Reformation histories.

But from the perspective of Luther himself, the very same printing presses that allowed him to gain an immense reading public[2] also permitted the equally rapid spread of the writings of reformers with whom he vehemently disagreed. And although Luther died before John Calvin's rise to prominence, the printing of Calvin's systematic *Institutes of the Christian Religion* certainly helped spread the Reformed faith—which Lutherans detested—wider and farther than Lutheranism itself.

Nor did the printing press discriminate against the Catholic Church, which began turning out tracts of its own to promote the Catholic Counter-Reformation with detailed rebuttals of Luther's writings.

And just as the Reformation would not have occurred without the printing press neither would have the spread of modern atheism and secularism in the 1600s. Sadly, that isn't all the printing press allowed to burst into ever wider circulation. The 1500s also saw the first printings of pornographic novels, poems, and engravings.[3] This is not an old problem, but perennial, as we see in our own time. When people today praise the Internet for putting more information at our fingertips, they usually neglect to mention that perhaps the greatest commercial beneficiary of the Internet, besides brand names like Amazon and Google and eBay is pornography. One can argue that human nature, in this regard, doesn't change much.

Censorship developed accordingly. In fact, there has never been an era without censorship—it's merely a matter of who does the censoring (as one can see with the self-appointed, politically correct censoring of today). Censorship of printed material had already arisen prior to the Reformation, the pope setting up offices of censorship as early as 1475. In 1501 Pope Alexander VI "established preventive censorship in Germany...appointing three Electors along with the Archbishop of Magdeburg to control the publication of books." In the Fifth Lateran Council, Pope Leo X attempted to forbid the printing of books without ecclesiastical permission.[4] The Holy Roman Emperor soon did likewise, but since the individual principalities were ruled by their individual princes, those rulers on the side of Luther ensured that the reformers got their say,[5] though the reformers eventually and inevitably tried to ban each other's books and pamphlets.

Censorship was good for business, albeit inadvertently, because some publishers made a living by selling banned books. And publishers, over time, tended to be indiscriminate. Printers of Francophone Calvinist literature in the late 1500s, for example, later published the rabidly anti-Christian French *philosophes* of the 1700s, and a steady stream of pornography.[6]

Luther and the Printing Press

By December 1517—not even two months after Luther posted his *Disputation on the Power and Efficacy of Indulgences*—printers from Nuremberg, Leipzig, and Basel had issued separate editions.[7] Luther expressed surprise at this development. "It is a mystery to me how my theses...were spread to so many places. They were meant exclusively for our academic circle here.... They were written in such a language [Latin] that the common people could hardly understand them."[8]

Nevertheless, sales, and hence Luther's revolutionary influence, were enormous as more and more of his works were published:

Luther's stand against Rome aroused huge popular enthusiasm in the Empire and in German-speaking lands. A seemingly endless variety of individual acts of revolt against the old Church fed off his phenomenal volume of words rushing off the printing presses in German and Latin. There were 390 editions of various of Luther's writings published in Germany in 1523 alone, and it has been calculated that beyond what he himself had written, around three million copies of related pamphlets…were printed in German by 1525; Wittenberg's puny economy now boomed solely because of the sudden growth in its printing industry.[9]

Gutenberg and the Printing of Indulgences

We might assume, then, that Johannes Gutenberg, the inventor of the movable type printing press, was a pre-Reformation Lutheran mainly interested in printing great stacks of Bibles. But in fact Gutenberg (1398–1468) was a Catholic layman, not a reformer, and (rather ironically) the "first dated printed product from Gutenberg's workshop was an indulgence" issued from the archbishopric of Mainz (c. 1454).[10]

Indeed, to add to the irony, the printing press was a major cause of the Reformation not just because it rapidly spread Luther's protests but because prior to that it rapidly spread the sale of, and the abuse of, indulgences. Even before 1500, indulgences were a big business that enriched printers, middlemen distributors, salesmen, and the Church,[11] and as their sale became easier and more lucrative because of the printing press, their sales, and the abuse of indulgences, swelled to become the scandal that Luther protested.

If that weren't enough irony, the sales methods that promoted indulgences were were also used in selling tracts that condemned indulgences. Elizabeth Eisenstein quips, "A resort to promotional literature and high pressure salesmanship which characterized the tactics of indulgence sellers, such as Tetzel, also characterized schemes developed by early reformers such as Beatus Rhenanus to publicize Luther's attacks on indulgence-selling."[12] For printers, then, Reformation theology and profit went hand in hand.[13]

Part of that profit came from the development of the eight-page pamphlet. Many of these (written in German) promoted Lutheran protest or doctrine. As historian Mark Edwards notes,

> These pamphlets were handy, relatively cheap, readily concealed and transported, and accordingly well suited for delivering their message to a large popular audience. They could be easily transported by itinerant peddlers, hawked on street corners and in taverns, advertised with jingles [just like indulgences] and intriguing title pages, and swiftly hidden in a pack or under clothing when the authorities made an appearance. They were ideal for circulating a subversive message right under the noses of the opponents of reform.[14]

These pamphlets were called *Flugschriften* in German, "flying writings," which gives us a kind of proportionate grasp of the speed with which they could be produced and with which they traveled.

They had much the same subversive effect that the Internet has today on the "official" media, and in Luther's time, were immensely helpful to his cause.

The Printing Press and Luther's Protestant Enemies

But the press was also helpful to the cause of those Protestants who almost immediately parted ways with Luther. During the period between 1518 and 1525, Luther's publications sold by far the most of all the evangelical reformers. During this period, there were more than two hundred editions of Luther's various works, but almost fifty editions of his sworn Protestant enemy, Andreas von Karlstadt, whose views were in line with the development of the radical Reformation, particularly the Anabaptists. There were also thirty-four German editions of Huldrych Zwingli's works, which signaled a fundamental and permanent break between Lutherans and Zwinglians. There were ten editions of the radical Thomas Müntzer's writings. Müntzer was an early a protégé of Luther whom Luther called "the archdevil" for stirring up political revolution based upon Luther's own principles.[15] Müntzer answered in kind, calling Luther "Dr. Liar," who, against the demands of the gospel, took the side of the godless rich against the poor, and further, called Luther's "justification by faith alone" an "invented doctrine."[16] In print, of course.

During Luther's lifetime, the sheer bulk of his output was still far larger than those Protestants with whom he disagreed. In this regard, we should also mention that Catholic printings in German between 1518 and 1544 fell far behind the output of Luther's by a ratio of about five to one.[17] Yet, as the Reformation continued beyond Luther's life, the scales of publication would tip toward non-Lutheran interpretations of reform. Whereas Luther's writings were impassioned but not systematic, the writings of John Calvin were both, and hence his *Institutes of the Christian Religion* spread the Reformed Calvinist understanding of Protestantism much farther than Luther's. While the *Institutes* appeared in Latin, it also appeared in successive French editions between 1541 and 1560, and since French (through the success of the Valois and then Bourbon dynasties in expanding French power and influence) was becoming the *lingua franca* of Europe, Calvin's systematic *Institutes* proved a decisive gain for the Reformed branch of Protestantism over Lutheranism. A German translation in 1572 helped to ensure that Calvinism would be a significant factor in the Thirty Years' War in Germany.[18]

The Printed Vernacular Bible and End of Sola Scriptura

Readers might think that Luther's doctrine of *sola scriptura* was the cause of the printing of ever more Bibles (especially in the vernacular, since a Latin Bible is a difficult foundation upon which to build this doctrine effectively). This is true, of course, but fails to take account of how the printing of Bibles *led* to the doctrine of *sola scriptura—and* its destruction.

Luther provided his own translation of the New Testament into German, published in 1522. It was not, however, the first time the Bible, or parts of it, had been translated into the vernacular. A French translation of the Bible (obviously not printed) appeared in 1235, and in the 1400s, the first century of printing, vernacular translations were available in Dutch, Saxon, French, English,

Italian, Spanish, and Bohemian.[19] These vernacular translations not only spread lay readership of the Bible, but also (and importantly) helped to reinforce the rise of nationalism through establishing national languages.[20] The first German Bible to appear in print came from the extremely busy presses at Strasbourg more than a quarter century before Martin Luther was born.[21]

That helps us understand Luther's situation in 1522. It isn't that German translations didn't exist, but that they needed improvement *and* the reader needed guidance to avoid misreading the text. It was at about this time that Luther was wrestling with the Zwickau prophets, those who zealously took up Luther's cause, but had fundamental disagreements with the master, and with Zwingli in Switzerland who had already marked out his distance from Luther's interpretation of the Bible.

We see why Luther didn't just print the New Testament alone, but included his interpretive commentary. As Mark Edwards notes, "Concerned by what he viewed as misreadings of the sacred text, and alarmed by the misunderstandings found among those now professed to be his supporters, Luther arrayed within his *German New Testament* a panoply of techniques to guide the reading of this crucial text.... The authority of 'Scripture alone' was being subtly subverted by printing itself."[22]

Luther's preface makes the case that while "It would only be right and proper if this volume [of the New Testament] were published without any preface," the difficulty is that "many unscholarly expositions and introductions have perverted the understanding of Christian people till they have not an inkling of the meaning of the gospel as distinct from the law, the New Testament as distinct from the Old Testament."[23]

In setting out this preface and his individual prefaces to the various books of the New Testament, Luther was engaged in the tacit admission that *sola scriptura* needed alongside it an authoritative interpretation, which was a roundabout admission of something like the Catholic understanding of *traditio* governing the understanding of the Bible. He further embedded the Lutheran *traditio* in the New Testament itself by his translation decisions, as well as in the glosses running down the side of the texts.

We must pause to grasp the deep historical and theological irony here. Luther's central assertion against the Catholic Church was that the Bible *alone* was the entirely sufficient foundation of Christianity, and that the Church's insistence on an authoritative interpretation *handed down* (*tradere* in Latin) with Scripture was a smokescreen keeping readers from the pure and simple biblical text. In his own translation of the Bible he was admitting, although perhaps not to himself, that authoritative interpretation did need to be handed down, albeit not the *traditio* of the Catholic Church but his own.

What was his *traditio*? It was one that took "justification by faith alone" as the central interpretative doctrine of the Bible. "The true kernel and marrow of all the books, those which should rightly be ranked first, are the gospel of John and St. Paul's epistles, especially that to the Romans, together with St. Peter's first epistle," Luther informed the reader. That meant a kind of "downgrading" of other aspects of the New Testament. "It follows that the gospel of John is unique in loveliness, and of a truth the principal gospel, far, far superior to the other three, and much to be preferred. And in the same way, the epistles of St. Paul and St. Peter are far in advance of the three gospels of Matthew, Mark, and Luke." On the very bottom, barely making it into the New Testament, there was "the epistle of St. James" which Luther declared, "is an epistle full of straw, because it contains nothing evangelical."[24]

The Gospel, for Luther, really meant the Gospel of John as understood through his reading of St. Paul. He downgraded the other three Gospels because they had a marked tendency to speak of the things that Jesus Christ demanded Christians *do* in order to inherit eternal life.

There was already a complaint against Luther's tendency to upgrade and downgrade books of the Bible, especially his desire to drop the Epistle of James completely, a position he'd stated earlier on. This complaint wasn't from a papist but from one of his own followers gone rogue, Karlstadt, who in 1520 warned Luther, "If it is permissible to make something great or little as one pleases, it will happen at last that the dignity and authority of [biblical] books depends on our power. And then, by whatever right any Christian is allowed to reject my ideas, I have the same right...to esteem my own highly and trample down those of others.... Brother, I beg you, am I not able to say the same about all scripture if I follow you?"[25]

Of course, Catholic opposition to Luther's translation, prefaces, and glosses arose soon after publication, the principal one being by Hieronymus Emser, at the behest of Duke Georg of Albertine Saxony. The duke demanded his subjects turn over copies of Luther's New Testament. Emser's work was to show line by line, gloss by gloss, why Luther's translation and his interpretation were faulty and hence misleading to the faith. Published in 1523, it had the catchy title *On What Grounds and for What Reason Luther's Translation of the New Testament Should Properly Be Forbidden to the Common Man.*[26]

It's fair to say that Luther's New Testament translation won out over Emser's attempt to quell it. By 1525 almost 80 percent of German pamphlets quoting the New Testament used Luther's translation, including many German Catholic pamphlets attacking him.[27]

But again, other Protestants attacked Luther too, using Scripture, of course. Karstadt, for instance, challenged Luther's scriptural support for affirming the understanding of the Eucharist as a sacrament. As a proto-Anabaptist, Karlstadt insisted that the bread and wine were only symbols, the position taken by Zwingli as well.

A battle of the Bible ensued, with Karlstadt in 1525 firing off a pamphlet titled *Exegesis of These Words of Christ: This Is My Body, Which Will Be Given for You. This Is My Blood, Which Will be Poured Out for You. Luke 22. Against the One-Fold and Two-Fold Papists Who Use Such Words for the Demolition of Christ's Cross.*[28] Karlstadt provided his own exegesis of Scripture, seasoned with epithets for Luther and his supporters, calling them "new papists," "blind guides," "dizzy spirits," "double papists," "the Anti-Christ's late-born friend," and most notably, the "malicious assassin of the Scripture."[29]

The distinct branches of Protestantism would each develop distinct written confessions, statements of their *traditio* that signaled the end of *sola scriptura* in fact if not in theory. This trend would continue and escalate for the rest of Luther's life and beyond. The Lutherans produced the *Augsburg Confession* (1530), the Reformed Church produced the *Heidelberg Catechism* (1563), the Anglican Church produced the *Thirty-Nine Articles* (1571), and the Anabaptists produced *The Schleitheim Confession* (1527). Each confession was a statement of the right way to understand

Scripture, against rival interpretations, thereby showing that Scripture alone was an insufficient guide.

The Unfortunate Catholic Response

In the year of Luther's death, 1546, the Catholic reform council of Trent declared what it considered to be the orthodox canon of Scripture, including the books from the Old Testament that Protestants had rejected, Tobit, Judith, Wisdom of Solomon, Ecclesiasticus (Sirach), Baruch, I and II Maccabees, and some material from Daniel and Esther.

It also ordained and declared "that the old Latin Vulgate Edition" must be "held as authentic," and that no one "may presume to interpret them [the Scriptures] contrary to the sense which holy mother Church, to whom it belongs to judge of their true sense and interpretation, has held and holds...." Against those "printers...who, now without restraint, thinking what pleases them is permitted them, print without the permission of ecclesiastical superiors the books of the Holy Scriptures and the notes and commentaries thereon of all persons indiscriminately," the Church warns that all such printing must be examined and approved by Church officials.[30]

Needless to say, this statement was made against the multiplication of vernacular translations that had occurred under the push of the doctrine of *sola scriptura*, and even more, the multiplication of commentaries and glosses on the Bible, such as Luther's, that had taken rival doctrinal positions even among Protestants. The fact that there were, by this time, irreparable divisions among Protestants, all of whom appealed to the principle of *sola scriptura*, made the Catholic Church all the more cautious in allowing the laity to take advantage of the flow of Bibles from presses all over Europe.

Yet we should be aware that there was debate in the Council of Trent itself over translation into the vernacular, those cautiously affirming it arguing that the real problem was the need for reform within the Church, especially in the education of the clergy.[31] The Council, in declaring for the official Vulgate, did not explicitly reject vernacular translations (since translations had been done under its auspices before the Reformation broke out). But in 1564, Pope Pius IV did declare that,

> We have learned by experience that if the sacred books, translated into the vernacular, are indiscriminately circulated, there follows because of the weakness of man more harm than good. In this matter the judgment of the bishop or the inquisitor must be sought, who on the advice of the pastor or the confessor may permit the reading of the Bible translated into the vernacular by Catholic authors. This may be done with the understanding that from this reading no harm, but an increase of faith and piety, results. The permission must be in writing. But he who dares to read or possess Scripture without this permission cannot receive absolution from his sins until he has returned the Bible to the ordinary.[32]

This caused the wholly unfortunate tendency within the Catholic Church to keep the Bible away from the Catholic laity, a tendency that took a very long time to reverse.

The Printing of the Polyglot: Return to the Original Languages

One might be misled by the just-quoted statement of Pope Pius IV that the Catholic Church had done everything it could up until that point, and then beyond, to keep the lid on any attempts to study Scripture in depth. Precisely the opposite is the case.

It's certainly well enough known that even before Luther, the Renaissance humanists had thrown themselves into the rediscovery of ancient languages, in particular, Hebrew and Greek, but also Aramaic, the original languages of the Bible. The zeal for studying these languages was part of the deep desire to uncover the riches of Holy Scripture in the original, and provide improved translations, initially in Latin.

We often hear of the Catholic humanist Erasmus in this regard, since his 1516 edition of New Testament in Greek and Latin on facing pages, was so mightily influential in unseating confidence in the Latin Vulgate, and in turning Protestants (including Luther himself) into biblical scholars and translators. As Erasmus makes clear in the foreword to the third edition (1522), he undertook these labors because he "would like to see it [the New Testament] turned into all the languages there are."[33] Despite his original view that the simple truths of the Gospel would thereby shine through, and in light of the fact that Luther himself had used Erasmus' Greek for his own translation of the New Testament into German, Erasmus was soon locked into debate with Luther about the interpretation of Scripture in regard to free will (1525, with the Catholic Erasmus in favor of free will and Luther opposed on the Protestant grounds of "predestination"), a debate read all over Europe. The printing press made this all possible.

Erasmus' New Testament was not, however, the first scholarly attempt to recover the original languages. A far more thorough, far more scholarly work, the *Complutensian Polyglot Bible*, had been underway since 1502 under the auspices of the Catholic Church, a project financed and overseen by Francisco Ximenes de Cisneros, a Spanish cardinal. This massive six-volume work included both the Old and New Testaments, with side-by-side columns of Hebrew, Latin, and Septuagint Greek, with Aramaic on the bottom of the Old Testament, and side-by-side Greek and Latin for the New Testament. The sixth volume included dictionaries of all the original languages. Erasmus used the Greek of the *Complutensian Polyglot* for his own 1516 edition by permission from the pope. In fact, the publishing arrangements therein caused the delay of the printing of the *Polyglot* until 1520, even though it was ready to go in 1517.

In the printed Dedicatory Prologue to the *Polyglot*, addressed to Pope Leo X, Cardinal Ximenes stated,

> There are many reasons, Holy Father, that impel us to print the languages of the original text of Holy Scripture. These are the principal ones. Words have their own unique character, and no translation of them, however complete, can entirely express their full meaning. This is especially the case in that language [Aramaic] which the Lord Himself spoke.... Moreover, wherever there is a diversity in the Latin manuscripts or the suspicion of a corrupted reading (we know how frequently this occurs because of the ignorance and negligence of copyists), it is necessary to go back to the original source of Scripture,

as St. Jerome and St. Augustine and other ecclesiastical writers advise us to do, to examine the authenticity of the books of the Old Testament in the light of the correctness of the Hebrew text and of the New Testament in the light of the Greek copies.[34]

Cardinal Ximenes ends, "May your Holiness receive, therefore, with a joyful heart this humble gift which we offer unto the Lord so that the hitherto dormant study of Holy Scripture may now at last begin to revive."[35] And so it did, both Catholic and (soon enough) Protestant. Luther's own translation of the New Testament in 1522 relied on Erasmus' Greek, and hence on the Catholic *Complutensian Polyglot Bible*.

The return to the original languages did not (as Erasmus had hoped) yield a universality of interpretation based upon a simple Gospel that lay beneath. The reasons weren't entirely the result of the rival Catholic, Lutheran, Zwinglian, Anglican, Anabaptist, and then Calvinist doctrinal disagreements that would soon arise. Cardinal Ximenes himself pinpointed additional causes for difficulties in his Prologue: (1) the words of the original languages have their own "unique character" which makes it difficult to translate them into other vernaculars, and (2) there are a variety of manuscripts which, because of copying problems, contain variant original readings. The more manuscripts that were discovered, the more variant readings multiplied and had to be dealt with by scholars.

So it was that the printing press brought about not just a flood of different vernacular Bibles, but also a growing stream of scholarly biblical studies trying to sort out different textual readings set forth in successive polyglot Bibles and lesser publications. The aim of all Christians of good will was to get to the best original language text and then produce the best translation. The modern disciples of Lucretius, however, saw the whole enterprise quite differently: as a proof that revelation itself was built on sandy ground. They sensed that biblical controversy could help them hasten the demise of Christianity.

CHAPTER ELEVEN

The Reformation Led to a Pagan Counter-Attack on the Bible

†he printing press led not just to a battle of the books when it came to the rival biblical interpretations of Catholics, Lutherans, Zwinglians, Calvinists, and the rest, but to pagan attacks on the Bible itself *through* the medium of scriptural scholarship.

This very thorough attack on the Bible is one of the great sources of our contemporary secularized society. Enemies of Christianity well understood that they were not just attacking a set of doctrines or ecclesiastical structures, but a sacred book that provided the foundation for both Catholics and Protestants. Knock out Holy Scripture, and everything would fall.

As differences between Catholic, Lutheran, Zwinglian, Anglican, Anabaptist, and Calvinist interpretations of Holy Scripture
proliferated, secularists saw the Bible not just as a compendium of
superstition—easily disproven by materialist science that had no
place for miracles—but as a noxious source of political discord,
social unrest, and war.[1]

The odd thing about the secular-Lucretian attack on Scripture
is that most of it has been incorporated into what is called modern
historical critical scholarship, the mode of scholarship that one
learns in the Religion Departments of almost every university in
America and Europe. That's why today the inevitable effect of
attending classes on the Bible in nearly all our universities, or even
worse, getting a Ph.D. in Biblical Studies, is the inculcation of deep,
systematic unbelief in the student. Those who go in, assuming that
they will learn more about their Christian faith by studying the
Bible with experts, come out on the other side as complete skeptics,
zealous to inculcate unbelief in others.

We are thereby faced with the irony that, five hundred years
after the Reformation, the most authoritative source of skepticism
about the Bible in our culture is the academic biblical scholar. To
understand how the hermeneutical foxes got to be in charge of the
scriptural studies henhouse, we need to return to the time of Luther
and then move forward.

Machiavelli, Descartes, and Thomas Hobbes: The Grandfathers of Modern Scriptural Scholarship

We recall that the atheist Machiavelli, a contemporary of
Luther, was deeply influenced by the pagan notion that religion

was a ruler's ruse, a fiction used to control the ignorant masses. Machiavelli didn't just float this idea by the reader. He actually turned to Scripture itself, and used the Bible to illustrate the pagan take on religion. In his *The Prince* and *Discourses on the First Ten Books of Titus Livy*, he infused his readers with this notion by treating Moses as one more secular prince who understood the necessity of pretending the he had direct contact with a god so that he had divine sanction for his own humanly-contrived laws. In other words, he implied that Moses chiseled his own command-ments on tablets while he was on Mount Sinai—during a propi-tious thunderstorm!—and foisted them on the gullible Jews so he could more easily rule them.[2]

Thus, Machiavelli's exegesis of the Bible was defined by his aim of showing rulers of his day that Christianity was merely *one more religion* that can be treated as Plutarch, Livy, and Polybius had treated ancient Greek and Roman religion—as a false but useful political instrument. Machiavelli's writings spread across Europe at the same as Luther's, which amounted to a one-two punch against the Catholic Church.

Printing presses were also turning out new editions of the ancient pagan philosophers themselves. These too were snatched up and zealously read—Lucretius' *On the Nature of Things* as well the writings as his mentor Epicurus, Lucian's *The Lover of Lies* and *The Passing of Peregrinus*, Cicero's *On the Nature of the Gods* and *On Divination*, and the works of Livy, Polybius, and Plutarch on which Machiavelli relied for his pagan treatment of Christianity.

All of these works helped reinforce the Machiavellian pagan rereading of Scripture. To these, we must add the works of Averroes and Marsilius and of newly minted skeptics who, by the late seventeenth century were circulating works like the clandestine text *The Three Impostors*, which ridiculed Moses, Jesus, and Muhammad as crafty, disingenuous Machiavellians who invented their respective religions to rule over superstitious fools. What Machiavelli implied, *The Three Impostors* took as a fact so that religion could be completely dismissed.

René Descartes (1596–1650) did not offer his own exegesis of Scripture, but by promoting a philosophy of mathematical-mechanical materialism, which implied that the Bible, with its miracles, had to be taken on irrational faith—a position he stated with Machiavellian circumspection.[3] In doing so, he gave skeptics more reason to assert that faith, and the Bible, was itself irrational. That's why philosopher Richard Popkin concluded that "Modern philosophy issuing from Cartesianism and modern irreligion issuing from Bible criticism" have a common source in Descartes.[4]

We next come to unconscionably long-lived Thomas Hobbes (1588–1679), one of England's most notorious atheists,[5] who was also the "father of modern scriptural scholarship."[6] Hobbes was not a disciple of Jesus Christ, but of Epicurus and Lucretius, and a zealous proponent of materialist atomism. He was quite aware of the work of Descartes, and openly rejected the Frenchman's dualism of spirit and matter (which was what allowed Descartes to profess his fideism), rightly seeing the spirit part as entirely redundant to Descartes' mechanistic explanations.[7] The motion of material atoms, for Hobbes, explained everything.[8] Yet, at the same time, Hobbes adopted Machiavelli's approach to religion: the pagans were right; it was a useful instrument for rulers to control the ruled.[9]

Thus, Hobbes didn't attack Christianity as an open atheist, but cleverly reformulated Christianity for his purposes through a convoluted and ingenious exegesis of Scripture itself (hence the "father of modern scriptural scholarship" tag). Much of Hobbes' most famous work, *The Leviathan* (1651), is dedicated to this task.

His first step was to affirm that Christianity is a matter of faith because God is incomprehensible by our reason,[10] and that this irrational faith must be rooted in Scripture. His goal was not to advance the Protestant doctrine of *sola scriptura*, but (with the same intent as Machiavelli and Marsilius) to subordinate the interpretation of Scripture to the state, putting the absolute power over religion *and* of scriptural interpretation into the hands of the king.[11] He does this through a long, elaborate, and often tedious exegesis of the Old and New Testament, which makes use of the newest scholarship of the day, "demonstrating" that the Bible itself shows that the interpretation of the Bible is entirely the civil sovereign's prerogative. He also discovers that all citizens are also commanded by Scripture to render unto Caesar full obedience (citing especially the passages of St. Paul that stress obedience to civil authority).[12]

We must add too all this, something that strikes the reader of Hobbes' *Leviathan*—its insistently anti-Catholic tone and substance. This was no pretense. Hobbes really did hate Catholics, primarily because Catholicism pulled the political allegiance of subjects away from the king and toward Rome. But, good Machiavellian that he was, Hobbes was also astute enough to take advantage of the Protestant diatribes against scheming popes, crafty priests, and malignant monks, so that he could yoke the anti-Catholic sentiment and rhetoric to *his* version of *sola scriptura* and obedience to Caesar (both likewise borrowed from Protestantism).

Through Hobbes' exegetical ministrations, the Bible becomes the political instrument of an absolutist king, advancing his cause through the Protestant doctrine of *sola scriptura* and the political doctrine of *cuius regio, eius religio* (which had been re-enunciated three years earlier at the close of the Thirty Years' War), thus turning Reformation theological principles toward entirely secular ends.

The Enlightenment *philosophes*, whether Deists or atheists, who followed in Hobbes' wake, also used his tactics, borrowing from a plethora of Protestant polemics against evil popes, lecherous clergy, and morally degraded monks and nuns, as a means to deliver de facto anti-Christian, Lucretian arguments.

Today we're so used to having anti-Christian rhetoric put in the form of parodies of Protestant Bible-thumping Southern Baptists that we may not realize that parodies of statue-worshipping, superstition-mongering, dragon-riding, Babylonian papal whores served the same purpose in the 1600s and 1700s. The skeptics well understood that they could exploit Christian divisions to destroy Christianity.

The *Other* Father of Modern Scriptural Scholarship, Benedict Spinoza

In his *Discourse on Method,* Descartes mentions his great appreciation of the Netherlands as a place where he was left alone in the midst of its commercial busyness and relatively tolerant attitude toward variations in religious belief.[13] Nearly half a century later, by the last part of the 1600s, the Netherlands was a magnet for the most radical Protestants who had taken the doctrine of *sola scriptura* and the *priesthood of all believers* to extremes that orthodox Lutherans and Calvinists, let alone Catholics, could not abide—Arminians who deviated from orthodox Calvinism, Anabaptist Mennonites, Socinians who rejected the Holy Trinity, and Quakers who seemed to reject the Bible itself for personal revelation of the inner light.

For this reason, the Netherlands also drew religious skeptics (especially Cartesians) and outright atheists. Into this milieu, Benedict Spinoza, a Jew, was born in 1632. By the time he was twenty-four, he was excommunicated by the rabbis of Amsterdam's Jewish community as a heretic. Such were the beginnings of the other father, after Hobbes, of modern scriptural scholarship.[14] Spinoza became the center of Europe's most radically anti-Christian intellectual circle, centered in the Netherlands.[15]

Spinoza was the direct intellectual disciple of Descartes, but also deeply influenced by Machiavelli and Hobbes, as well as Averroes. Rejecting Descartes' spirit-matter dualism as incoherent, he put forth in its place an entirely materialist pantheism wherein god was identified with nature, and nature with god. This, of course, was not the Christian God, but a philosophical one of Spinoza's own construction, creating a divinized nature and a naturalized deity.[16] Since this pantheism was so completely at odds with the Judeo-Christian understanding of God as entirely distinct from, and the Creator of, nature, wherever Spinoza's philosophy spread, Christianity declined accordingly.

But the obvious questions arise, *why* did Spinoza fabricate such an oddity, and *how* does that affect the interpretation of the Bible? To put it all in a nutshell, he constructed his pantheistic account of nature to undermine the Bible. Spinoza's "logic" goes like this. We all agree that god cannot contradict himself. If god is nature, and nature is god, then nothing in nature/god can contradict itself. Therefore, alleged miracles, which contradict the "laws" of nature/god, cannot have occurred. Since there cannot be any miracles, then scientific scriptural exegesis of the Bible must remove them.[17]

This train of assumptions and deductions occurs in Spinoza's most famous (infamous) book, the founding document of modern academic biblical scholarship, his *Theologico-Political Treatise*, published in 1670 and immediately condemned (and read) everywhere.[18]

As with Hobbes' *Leviathan*, Spinoza undermines Scripture through an intense, laborious exegesis of Scripture. This exegesis is, again, defined by the assumption that miracles cannot have occurred. Conjuring up natural explanations for the miracles found in the Old and New Testaments thus becomes the point of biblical scholarship. So, for example, the Red Sea wasn't miraculously parted by Moses, Spinoza explains, but happened to have been blown back by a propitious wind, the same kind of wind that had earlier (and likewise non-miraculously) brought locusts to plague Egypt. Elisha didn't actually raise a dead boy, but in lying on top of the unconscious lad, warmed him up enough to revive him. Something about the mixture of spit and dust, used by Christ, brought about the medicinal, not miraculous, cure of the blind man. The sun didn't really stand still for Joshua to do battle; it just *seemed* that way because the battle was a long one. And so on. Spinoza informs his readers that one mustn't take all this characteristic Jewish hyperbole literally.[19]

But, Spinoza concedes, sometimes, no matter how clever the scriptural exegete, "there will be times when the text cannot be salvaged by finesse." The honest scientific exegete must then assume that the miraculous episode "was inserted in Sacred Writ by sacrilegious human beings. For whatever is contrary to nature is contrary to reason; and what is contrary to reason is absurd, and therefore refutable as well."[20] Why are these miracle-believing, Scripture-manipulating human beings "sacrilegious"? Because (as Spinoza's strange logic dictates) god is nature, and nature is god, and these religious reprobates are profanely declaring that nature/god can contradict its own laws! Attributions of the miraculous are now declared by Spinoza to be the height of blasphemy.

Further, according to Spinoza, the Bible is not a scientific or a philosophical book, but one written in a style that is appropriate for the ignorant lower classes. It's not inspired by the Holy Spirit, but the "spirit of the plebs," dealing with "only very simple matters, which can be perceived even by the slowest."[21] It doesn't teach the truth (Spinoza's pantheistic materialism), but it does offer salutary moral exhortations, the chief of which can be boiled down to "love of neighbor," which means, for Spinoza, *be nice, and let other people alone, no matter what they believe.*[22] So, Christians, stop fighting each other, and also, for godless' sake, stop pestering atheists! Scripture so redefined thereby becomes the instrument of the ruling elite of liberal democracy; in Spinoza's philosophy who are able to use the new and improved interpretation of the Bible to keep Christian subjects tame and docile.[23] And so we have, with Spinoza, yet another form of modern Averroism, which would have made Marsilius and Machiavelli proud.

To make sure that Scripture cannot be revived and used with the irrational, impassioned Christian multitude, Catholic or Protestant, Spinoza set forth as one of the additional tasks of the new scientific exegete, the maximizing of confusion about the real meaning of the text, by ferreting out all the possible ambiguities inherent in the original languages, and by displaying prominently all the variations that occur in the multiple manuscripts discovered since the Renaissance—and, of course, publishing the results. It's hard for the Bible to have authority if we can't figure out what it actually said originally. Better just to mind your own business, and embrace tolerance.

The very scholarly apparatus that both Catholics and Protestants believed would take them closer to the revealed truth, and bring about ever more accurate translations of God's Holy Word, thereby became the vehicle Spinoza and his followers used to sow confusion and doubt, leading to the secularization of the West.

CHAPTER TWELVE

The Thirty Years' War That Followed the Reformation Was (Wrongfully) Used to Discredit Christianity

The Thirty Years' War was not just a horrifying incident in its own right, but also became a set propaganda piece for the secular-minded who viewed religion as *the* cause of human misery. They could have no better and bloodier weapon at their disposal in the Enlightenment than the three-decade-long carnage marking the first half of the seventeenth century. So it would seem, until we take a closer look at the war itself, rather than merely repeat the charge. When we do, we'll find out that things are considerably more complex.

Certainly, religious differences played a part in the war, but imperial aims, dynastic ambitions, nationalist fervors and rivalries, antagonisms between classes, hope for territorial or material gain, and the fear and jealousy of petty princes were more than enough to bring about and sustain the war regardless of divisions between Protestants and Catholics. The history of Europe before and after the Reformation was rife with wars over political or nationalist ambitions. The Thirty Years' War fits into that same category, which is why, in that war, we find the Catholic king of France subsidizing a Lutheran general to fight a Catholic emperor; Catholic France fighting Catholic Spain; Lutherans siding with Catholics against Calvinists; a pope opposed to a Catholic emperor; nobles and petty princes choosing their religion based upon political strategy; and mercenaries who will fight for anybody, as long as they are handsomely rewarded.

This Land Is Your Land, This Land Is My Land: Dynastic Claims

During this period of European history, cities, regions, and even nations, and the people in them, were passed on to aristocratic heirs like houses and furniture. If you think family squabbles over grandma's kitchen tables and chairs can get ugly, think about locking horns over who gets the Netherlands, or Bohemia, or pieces of Italy, or even all of Germany.

Germany was the battleground in the Thirty Years' War (1618–1648) that involved the Spanish imperial Habsburgs, the Austrian Habsburgs, the German Electoral Princes, countless lesser German nobles, France, the Netherlands, Sweden, and the pope. But we must make clear before moving on, that when we speak of Germany, there actually wasn't one at the time. Instead of a centralized state, it was a crazy quilt of principalities. As S. H. Steinberg notes:

To speak of "Germany" as if it were the central European equivalent of France or Spain or Sweden, is a deceptive but convenient simplification. In reality, "the German section of the Holy Roman Empire," as was its official title, consisted of the patched-up relics of the medieval Empire, in which the age-old antagonism between the Emperor and the princes, the rivalry between the privileged group of electoral princes and the lesser princes, the quarrels between the princes and the representative Estates, and other feuds had, during the sixteenth century been overlaid and exacerbated by religious divisions.[1]

The Holy Roman Emperor and His Expanding (and Shrinking) Empire

At the time of the Reformation, the Holy Roman Empire was bordered to the west by France, to the east by Poland and Bohemia, and stretched (roughly speaking) from the top of Italy to the North Sea and the Baltic Seas (excluding Denmark). The empire was under the dynastic control of the Habsburgs, rich landowners originating in Austria. The emperor was a quasi-national king but with power and territory distributed among lesser nobles who more or less shared a common language. The Habsburgs were exceedingly deft at marrying their way into dynastic dowries, getting the Low Countries in the north, Franche-Comté (Burgundy) in the west, Luxembourg, and a very important union with the daughter of Ferdinand and Isabella of Spain. Charles V, who became Holy Roman Emperor in 1519 through this latter union, was a Spaniard with enormous imperial claims—not just Spain, the Low Countries, Austria, Franche-Comté, and what we call Germany, but all of Italy south of the Papal States (the Kingdom of Naples), the Islands of Corsica and Sardinia, Milan, Bohemia, and Hungary, as well as, via Spanish conquest and conversion, the newly discovered Americas, which supplied the Habsburgs with enormous piles of gold and silver. Things were starting to look truly imperial for the Habsburgs rather than merely Germanic-Spanish. It was time, so they thought, to finally make good on their universal imperial claims.

By every measure, Charles V, the greatest Holy Roman Emperor since Charlemagne, was an ardent and sincere Catholic. He was also one of Luther's most powerful opponents, but his opposition to Protestantism was inseparable from his imperial ambition to create a united Europe with one emperor and one faith. Perhaps needless to say, France, the Papal States, the Republic of Venice, Denmark, many of the German princes, and other powers great and small, however Catholic (or not) they might be, were less enamored of this imperial ideal. The pope, of course, was all in favor of Catholicism, but not of becoming the political vassal of the Holy Roman Emperor. To much of the rest of Europe, it looked like a Spanish king was going to enforce Spanish rule for the sake of the Spanish Habsburgs with Spanish Catholicism as the state religion.

It is these nationalist and great-power conflicts that explain why Charles V's campaign against the Lutheran Princes of the Schmalkaldic League in 1546–1547 was thwarted by the Catholic French Valois monarchy throwing its weight behind the Lutherans; why the Lutheran Duke Moritz of Saxony fought variously *for* the Empire, and, in alliance with Catholic France, *against* the Empire; and why, though religion did play a role here, the Schmalkaldic

League excluded non-Lutheran Protestants. Politics were more important than religion.

At the end of his reign, Charles conceded that imperial unity was impossible, and with the Peace of Augsburg in 1555 consented to the principle of *cuius regio, eius religio,* dividing the empire between the Catholic and Lutheran princes (and, incidentally but purposely, excluding Calvinists and Anabaptists). Charles resigned as emperor in 1556, betaking his exhausted self to a monastery, and his vast holdings were divided between the Spanish and Austrian possessions, the former handed to his son, Philip II, as king of Spain, and the latter to Charles's younger brother, Ferdinand, as Holy Roman Emperor.

By 1600, Spain had gone into steep decline (disguised to an extent by its excellent military) and the Germanic Holy Roman Empire remained a patchwork, "divided into three hundred autonomous political units, of which at least three dozen had some importance. The real rulers of Germany were the local princes."[2]

Historian Richard Dunn further notes that in the sixteenth century,

> The German princes, Catholic and Lutheran, had in effect ganged up against the Habsburgs. They had observed, correctly enough, that Charles V had been trying not only to crush Protestantism but to increase Habsburg power and check the centrifugal tendencies [toward dissolution into lesser principalities] within the empire.... The princes, both Lutheran and Catholic, had also been trying to turn the Reformation crisis to their own personal advantage, by asserting new authority over

the local churches, tightening ecclesiastical patronage, and squeezing more profit from church revenues.[3]

While the imperial Habsburgs were in decline, France was on the rise. Since 1589, France had been led by the Bourbon dynasty, when Henry IV converted from Calvinism to Catholicism to become king. Elsewhere, Calvinism was on the march. By the early 1600s, two of the three Protestant Imperial Electors were Calvinists and the third was Lutheran and strongly anti-Calvinist.[4] In 1608, Protestant princes formed the Protestant Union, which was counterbalanced the following year by a Catholic League. But these groupings were not entirely religious or entirely unified. The Catholic League, for instance, did not include Austria, the primary Catholic power of central Europe, and the Protestant Union was supported by the Catholic, albeit former Protestant, king of France (Henry IV) and was itself divided by enmity between Lutherans and Calvinists, with Calvinists "forming the great majority of its members."[5]

Tipping the balance of power in Europe was the sudden rise of Sweden under Gustavus Adolphus, who reigned from 1611 to 1632. Sweden was solidly Lutheran, though this was largely a political decision, as in England, allowing the state to seize church land,[6] and its Lutheranism was no hindrance to its fighting Lutheran Denmark for control of the lucrative Baltic trade. Gustavus Adolphus's army became one of the great armies of Europe. Without it, the Thirty Years' War wouldn't have lasted thirty years.

The war began when King Ferdinand of Bohemia, a Catholic crowned in 1617, tried to take away privileges from the Bohemian Protestant nobleman. The nobleman cornered two of Ferdinand's advisors at Hradschin Castle in Prague and defenestrated them.

After falling some fifty feet, they were saved by landing in a cushy pile of horse manure. This was the inauspicious beginning of the Bohemian revolt—a revolt that soon caught fire after the death of the Habsburg emperor Matthias in 1619. Of the seven Electoral Princes, three were Catholics (the archbishops of Mainz, Trier, and Cologne), and as we just noted, one was Lutheran (Saxony), and two were Calvinist (Brandenburg, and the Palatinate). The seventh Elector was the king of Bohemia. While the Protestant Electors could have blocked him from becoming emperor, they did not; but the Bohemian Protestant noblemen, in his absence, elected a Calvinist prince, Frederick, as Bohemia's king.

As S. H. Steinberg wryly notes, "The Bohemians could not have made a more unfortunate choice. Frederick was a pleasure-loving nonentity." His counselors from the Palatine encouraged him to force Calvinism on the Lutheran Bohemians—who detested Calvinism as much as Catholicism[7]—and to do so as "a religious fight for the gospel." To the Lutheran Bohemians, it appeared Frederick's ascension was a coup by the Bohemian nobility who were using Calvinism for political ends.[8]

The Bohemian revolt was soon squelched by a combination of Maximilian, the Catholic duke of Bavaria; Philip III of Catholic Spain; and the Lutheran Elector of Saxony. That should have been the end of the war, but it left the mercenary army of Ernst von Mansfield—a Catholic turned Calvinist and a man of fluid principles who "switched sides several times, always working for the highest bidder"[9]—looking for work after the demise of its Protestant patron. Mansfield took his army through Germany, pillaging and sacking along the away, chased by Maximilian of Bavaria who punished the Protestant populations he assumed were sympathetic to Mansfield.

These tactics help explain why the Thirty Years' War was so devastating to Germany. Large armies of, say, fifteen thousand could only stay in the field if they could live off other's land (soldiers have to eat) and relieve them of their money by extortion (soldiers have to be paid). Since there was only so much to take from any particular place, these armies had to continually move from one area to the next, thereby leaving a wake of destruction. In Gustavus Adolphus's words, *war must sustain war*, so that, as explained by historian Richard Bonney, "once an army had devastated the land it had occupied, it must move on to new territory where it could repeat the process."[10] For soldiers who were often given neither their promised pay nor their promised rations, and whose camps could become festering dens of dysentery, plunder was a way of life.[11] Letting soldiers loose on the locals helped retain their loyalty. Good commanders, noted one participant in the war, gave their troops "some liberty of booty: to the end that they might prove the more resolute another time, for Souldiers will not refuse to undergoe any hazard, when they see their Officers willing to reward them with honour and profit."[12] Religious differences weren't the cause of the carnage. Most of the damage done in the Thirty Year's War was done not in battle, but in the pillaging (and disease) that accompanied it, and the necessity of providing food and pay for the vast mercenary armies.

In 1625, Denmark entered the war, ostensibly to protect the Protestants in northern Germany from Maximilian's armies. But Emperor Ferdinand II had come to distrust Maximilian's political ambitions and decided to hire a mercenary commander of his own, Albrecht von Wallenstein.

Wallenstein was a Bohemian Protestant soldier of fortune who made a mint siding with the Catholic Ferdinand against the

Bohemian Protestants. Based on this success, Ferdinand appointed Wallenstein head of all imperial troops in April 1625. Wallenstein "was unscrupulous, greedy, reckless, cruel, quarrelsome, and superstitious,"[13] but nevertheless a gifted mercenary commander. Wallenstein was so successful that he not only defeated Ernst von Mansfield, but made his own putative allies, like Maximilian, indeed all the German princes, nervous, because "There seemed to be no reason why, with the help of Wallenstein's army, Ferdinand could not soon abrogate the whole Augsburg formula of 1555 and transform the empire into a Catholic absolute monarchy," a Habsburg take-all triumph.[14] The German Electors, Catholic and Protestant alike, pressed Ferdinand to dismiss Wallenstein, saying that he represented a potential threat to the emperor. Finally, reluctantly, the emperor capitulated and agreed to dismiss his highly successful general. It proved to be a tremendous mistake, because shortly thereafter, in 1630, Sweden decided to join the war against the empire, allied with the princes who feared the emperor's power, and itself "looking for conquest and profit."[15]

The armies of the Lutheran Swedish king and commander Gustavus Adolphus were subsidized by France's Cardinal Richelieu who put Catholic France's national interests in weakening the Empire well ahead of any religious consideration of supporting the Catholic Empire against its (mostly) Protestant enemies. For this reason, the Swedish king's advisors "expressly admonished" him "not to speak of a war of religion in the Protestant interest because 'the king of France would take umbrage.'"[16] Gustavus Adolphus pounded the imperial and Catholic League armies, and undid the effects of most of Wallenstein's victories.

Ferdinand then rehired his Protestant general, Wallenstein, to fight the Lutheran Swedes, and in a battle at Saxony in the fall of

1632, Gustavus Adolphus was killed. This might have ended the war, except for the fact that Wallenstein had no interest in ending the war, and rather more interest in auctioning his services to the highest bidder. The emperor sacked Wallenstein again, and Wallenstein was then assassinated in February 1634 by an Irish mercenary, Captain Walter Devereux.

The war continued as a feud between the Catholic Holy Roman Emperor and Catholic France, fought in Germany, with Swedish armies leading an allegedly Protestant cause, though France's only interest was in sapping the strength of the Habsburgs. "The war had become a Habsburg-Bourbon dynastic struggle, with the original religious, ethnic, and constitutional issues laid aside."[17] There were other battles as well, such as the Lutheran Swedes taking on their old enemies the Lutheran Danes (1643-1645) to wrest some land from Denmark.

The Peace of Westphalia (1648) finally sealed the Thirty Years' War by essentially repeating the conditions of the Peace of Augsburg (1555), except that now Calvinist rulers would join Catholic and Lutheran rulers in defining the religion of their realms. Anabaptists, their common enemy, were still excluded.

The result of the fighting: a devastated Germany, a weaker Holy Roman Emperor, some territory gained by France and Sweden, a shifting around of the borders and holdings of some of the German principalities—and a propaganda piece for Christianity's enemies who blamed Germany's devastation on the brutality generated by the ignorant, hateful superstitions of the faith.

Where was the pope in all this? It is true that Pope Urban VIII, who reigned for the bulk of the war (1623–1644), did little to broker a peace. Instead, he acted as a territorial prince. Historian S. H. Steinberg's bleak assessment was that Urban "was above all an

Italian prince interested in the technical aspects of war—he fortified Castel St. Angelo in Rome, set up a gun factory in Tivoli and transformed the Vatican library into an arsenal." Urban succeeded in protecting the Papal States from Habsburg encroachment but he certainly failed as a peacemaker who could reunite Christendom; indeed, it seemed that reuniting Christendom was not even his goal. Steinberg adds, "Whether Urban actively subsidized Gustavus Adolphus is a matter of dispute; he certainly welcomed the successes of the Swedish and French armies."[18] In the Thirty Years' War, even the pope cared less about advancing Catholicism than he did, as a territorial prince, about restraining the power of the Empire.

Reassessing the Thirty Years' War

Of necessity, I've offered only a bare bones account of an extremely complicated war—or series of wars—and left out much (including Spain's war in the Netherlands, which distracted Spain from using all its martial resources in Germany). But I trust we've done enough to see, quite clearly, that the Thirty Years' War was not, primarily, a religious war between Catholics and Protestants.

The real lesson of the Thirty Years' War is that in the seventeenth century, and indeed in the Reformation, nationalism and political ambition could be far more important than religion. The spirit of Machiavelli—and his *realpolitik* doctrine of *raison d'état* ("reason of State")—was more in the minds of many rulers and commanders than ideas of Christian unity or morality.[19] As S. H. Steinberg says, for example, of France,

> The emergence of France as the political and cultural
> leader of Europe [during this period of the Thirty Years'

War] was due largely to the fact that the French statesmen of the period—the Protestants [King] Henry IV and
Sully [Maximilien de Béthune, first duke of Sully, Henry's right-hand man], and the Catholics [Cardinals]
Richelieu and Mazarin—deliberately severed the traditional bond of religion and politics and made the novel
concept of *raison d'état* their guiding principle. The
exclusion of religious standards enabled France to
destroy Protestantism in France [the Huguenots] and to
secure religious and political uniformity at home and to
perpetuate the split of western Christendom [outside of
France]. Henceforth religious beliefs, orthodox or heretical, were increasingly confined to the sphere of personal
conviction and individual choice, whereas public affairs
were directed by a *raison d'état* which no longer needed
and used supernatural arguments for the pursuit of
worldly ends. [20]

In Steinberg's assessment, we have an apt summary of the significant shift, occurring within and directing the Thirty Years'
War, to a Machiavellian view of politics, one which uses religion
(Protestant or Catholic) as a political instrument, thereby giving
new life to the notion, found in Polybius and the other ancient
pagans, that religion was, after all, merely a useful fiction to be
manipulated by leaders for the own designs. If the ever-scheming
Cardinal Richelieu had really been, at heart, a devout Catholic he
wouldn't have done everything he could to ensure the fractioning
of Christianity outside of France, even while manipulating Catholicism as an instrument of political control and unity within France.

So much for the rulers, what about the soldiers? Were they informed primarily by religious beliefs? Here again, Steinberg clarifies. "The raising, training and employment of armies in the first half of the seventeenth century was in essence a large-scale, private enterprise industry. Both the officers and the men regarded military service as a means of making money and furthering their private interests." Their aims were not religious. "Love of adventure, hope of advancement, dissatisfaction or distress were the motives which induced men to flock to the standards raised by solvent entrepreneurs and to sell themselves to the highest bidder." It was a business, for both the leaders and the led, the officers and the infantry.[21] The main exception to this would be Gustavus Adolphus' army, at least in the initial phases. Absolutely not an exception were the likes of Sydnam Poyntz, an adventurous Englishman, who "changed both sides and religion but did not specifically match the two, enlisting with Protestant Saxony soon after his own conversion to Catholicism." When captured by the Catholic imperial armies, he joined them.[22]

The love of gain was not the preserve of mercenaries alone. We also find it among the nobles, such as the Catholic Maximilian of Bavaria who fought on the emperor's side, not primarily for the sake of the empire or Catholicism, but because (by secret agreement) Maximilian would receive significant parts of the Palatinate and even better, the electoral title would be transferred to the Wittelsbach dynasty, of which he was a part—the Wittelsbachs being the second greatest dynasty in Germany behind the Habsburgs. It was calculations of personal enrichment and political power, such as these, that in large part accounted for the duration and destruction of the war.

A proper view of the Thirty Years' War is one that sees it as one contested by Machiavellian rulers and mercenary soldiers. So if the war wasn't primarily a religious war—and it clearly wasn't— then how did it get to be one retrospectively? That, in itself, is an interesting story. In Steinberg's assessment, "The label of a 'war of religion' between Roman Catholics and Protestants has been attached to the 'Thirty Years War' by German writers whose philosophy of history was determined successively by the rationalism of the eighteenth, the liberalism of the nineteenth and the agnosticism of the twentieth century,"[23] all of which were informed by the fundamental Lucretian view that religion was *the* irrational cause of our human misery, and that progress meant the extirpation of religion.

In short, our picture of the Thirty Years' War is, in fact, one filtered through an Enlightenment propaganda campaign. Even people who have never heard of the Thirty Years' War have absorbed the idea that Christianity is a cause of division and hate and war, and hence is a pernicious superstition that can, at best, be tolerated only in its private expression. That, too, is one unfortunate outcome of the Reformation.

tHE ᑎEXt REFORᗰATIOᑎ

Since we know that reformations will never come to an end until the end, we may ask, what about the next reformation? As I hinted at the beginning, it seems certain that while Luther's Reformation led to a series of massive divisions in Christianity, the next reformation will lead to more Christian unity in the face of the combined threats of resurgent radical Islam and emboldened coercive secularism.

Every day, it seems, the newspaper juxtaposes stories that drive this point home. As I write, for instance, there has been another Islamist terror attack in England, with the Islamists aiming to strike at a Christian civilization (even if an increasingly secularized one). That same day I also read about a Catholic farmer in middle America who was denied access to a farmer's market because the locality was punishing him for "discrimination," in this case because he declined to host a homosexual wedding reception on his private property.

After the Islamist attack, many secularists (or what we might call liberals) issued calls for "tolerance" and "love," and vigorously denied that the terrorist attack had anything to do with Islam (despite the claims of the attackers themselves). But these same people expressed no sympathy for the Catholic farmer (just as we never hear a peep from them about the gruesome massacres of Christians in Islamic-dominated lands). The reason of course is that the secularists and the Islamists have the same enemy—Christianity and orthodox Christians. So while secularists will extend "tolerance" to their fellow anti-Christians the Islamists, they regard Christians as bigots who can be tolerated only if marginalized.

In such an atmosphere, orthodox Christians, Protestants, and Catholics, are almost inevitably going to find the theological issues that divide them less important than the Nicene Creed that unites them, disputes over the role of the papacy less important than the necessity of having a strong Christian voice in the world, arguments over biblical interpretation less important than upholding traditional biblical teaching.

Luther's Reformation was possible, in part, because, in a largely Christian society, there was an assumption that a revolution in Christian theology and practice would end with a still Christian, or even more Christian, society. But it didn't, and readers now understand more clearly why: radical secularism and radical Islam were there at the Reformation, both plotting the demise of

Christianity, and five hundred years later, they appear to be approaching their united goal.

So, we are in a much different world today than we were a half millennium ago, a world where Christianity is no longer the default way of understanding the world and our place in it, and Christians are under increasingly open assault by those who have been working to undermine their faith for centuries. That makes the *next* reformation crucial, one on which the continued existence of Christianity depends.

By this I do not mean to underplay the providential designs of God, who remains in control despite the best efforts of those manning the gates of hell to overcome the Church, and whose grace is necessary for the success of any efforts on our part. But just like the first apostles, the popes, St. Francis and St. Dominic, Martin Luther, Huldrych Zwingli, John Calvin, and all the other Protestant reformers, we face choices as Christians in the situation we happen to be in, and are responsible for prayerfully, humbly moving forward in the goal commanded by Jesus Christ, in the great mandate, to "make disciples of all the nations." That goal will be more fruitfully achieved in our own time if all Christians of good will move forward in ever-greater unity. Working toward that unity, which would bring the Reformation to a close, should define the spirit of the next reformation.

Acknowledgments

I'd like to thank Harry Crocker, the world's best editor, for once again doing a masterful job of cutting down an unwieldy manuscript into a wieldy book, and for all the other editing help of Nancy Feuerborn. I would also like to thank Franciscan University for providing extra help and support, and my family for understanding the difficulties of getting a book in on deadline.

Notes

Chapter One

1. For one of the most detailed studies see David Barrett and Todd Johnson, *World Christian Trends, AD 30–AD 2200: Interpreting the Annual Christian Megacensus* (Pasadena: William Carey, 2001). The relevant chapter on martyrdom is conveniently available on the Internet at http://www.gordonconwell.edu/ockenga/research/documents/WCT_Martyrs_Extract.pdf.

2. See ibid, and the summary at http://www.cesnur.org/2011/mi-cri-en.html.

3. John L. Allen Jr., *The Global War on Christians: Dispatches from the Front Lines of Anti-Christian Persecution* (New York: Image, 2013). Allen is relying on

the continuing research of Barrett and Johnson. See also George Marlin, *Christian Persecutions in the Middle East: a 21st Century Tragedy* (South Bend: St. Augustine's Press, 2015.

4. See its list at https://www.opendoorsusa.org/christian-persecution/world-watch-list/.

5. See Paul Marshall, Lela Gilbert, and Nina Shea, *Persecuted: The Global Assault on Christians* (Nashville: Thomas Nelson, 2013), ch. 2.

6. *Dei Verbum*, 22. Available at the Vatican website: http://www.vatican.va/archive/hist_councils/ii_vatican_council/documents/vat-ii_const_19651118_dei-verbum_en.html.

7. Available at the Vatican website: http://www.vatican.va/roman_curia/pontifical_councils/chrstuni/documents/rc_pc_chrstuni_doc_31101999_cath-luth-joint-declaration_en.html.

8. Lutheran World Federation and the Catholic Church, *Joint Declaration on the Doctrine of Justification*, 5.

9. Lutheran World Federation and the Catholic Church, *Joint Declaration on the Doctrine of Justification*, 7.

Chapter Two

1. *Didache*, ch. 11. There are, happily, many translations of the *Didache* online, including the one I'm using at http://www.earlychristianwritings.com/text/didache-roberts.html.

2. *Didache*, ch. 11.

3. *Didache*, ch. 12.

4. Edward Peters. *Heresy and Authority in Medieval Europe* (Council of Toulouse, 1229, Canon 14), 195.

5. To give a bit more information, Arianism is named after an early-fourth-century bishop, Arius, and claimed that Jesus Christ was not divine but created by the Father, a heresy against which the Nicene Council (325) and the consequent Nicene Creed were defined. Arianism is another kind of temptation, one that cannot abide by the central mystery of Christianity, the Most Holy Trinity. It is much easier, on the human mind, to affirm either one God or multiple gods. One God in Three Persons stretches beyond our merely human capacities. We don't like what we can't understand, so in regard to this central, defining Christian truth, the temptation is to remake Christianity in a humanly understandable form—to cut the God-man Jesus down to our size, and make him a fellow creature. St. Augustine battled Pelagianism in the early fifth century (a heresy named after a British monk Pelagius, a contemporary of Augustine). Pelagius held that the effects of the fall weren't all that bad, and in fact, we really could be good under our own efforts—a claim which St. Augustine realized would make Christ's Incarnation, death, and resurrection unnecessary. Good works, and not God's Grace, were all Pelagius thought were needed, at least by the superior sort of person.

6. Bronwen Neil and Matthew Dal Santo, *A Companion to Gregory the Great* (Leiden: Brill, 2013), Preface, xix.

7. Quoted in Bronwen Neil, "The Papacy in the Age of Gregory the Great," in Bronwen Neil and Matthew Dal

Santo, *A Companion to Gregory the Great*, 3–27, quote from 3.

8. Quoted in Brett Edward Whalen, *The Medieval Papacy* (New York: Palgrave Macmillan, 2014), 48.

9. Bronwen Neil, "The Papacy in the Age of Gregory the Great," 17.

10. Barbara Müller, "Gregory the Great and Monasticism," in Bronwen Neil and Matthew Dal Santo, *A Companion to Gregory the Great*, 83–108, esp. 97–98.

11. Cristina Ricci, "Gregory's Missions to the Barbarians," in Bronwen Neil and Matthew Dal Santo, *A Companion to Gregory the Great*, 29–56, quote from 44.

12. See Karl Baus, Hans-Georg Beck, Eugen Ewig, and Hermann Josef Vogt, *The Imperial Church from Constantine to the Early Middle Ages* (New York: Seabury, 1980), 406–11. This is Volume II of the series edited by Hubert Jedin and John Dolan, *Handbook of Church History*.

13. Quoted in Karl Baus, Hans-Georg Beck, Eugen Ewig, and Hermann Josef Vogt, *The Imperial Church from Constantine to the Early Middle Ages*, 631.

14. In John Moorhead, *Gregory the Great* (London and New York: Routledge, 2005), 74–87; quote from 79.

15. Bronwen Neil, "The Papacy in the Age of Gregory the Great," 17–22.

16. Constant J. Mews and Claire Renkin, "The Legacy of Gregory the Great in the Latin West," in Bronwen Neil and

Matthew Dal Santo, *A Companion to Gregory the Great*, 315–39, quote from 331.

17. See the overviews in Beverly Mayne Kienzle, "Religious poverty and the search for perfection," and Peter Biller, "Christians and heretics," both in Miri Rubin and Walter Simons, eds., *The Cambridge History of Christianity, Vol. 4: Christianity in Western Europe c. 1100–c. 1500* (Cambridge: Cambridge University Press, 2009), 39–53, 170–86.

18. These are the words of historian Roberto Ridolfi, quoted in John C. Olin, *The Catholic Reformation: Savonarola to Ignatius Loyola* (New York: Fordham University Press, 1992), 1.

19. Girolamo Savonarola, "On the Renovation of the Church," in John C. Olin, *The Catholic Reformation*, 4–15, quotes from 5–6.

20. Girolamo Savonarola, "On the Renovation of the Church," 8.

21. Girolamo Savonarola, "On the Renovation of the Church," 9, 13.

22. Eamon Duffy, *Saints & Sinners: A History of the Popes* (New Haven: Yale University Press, 2006, 3rd ed.), 177.

23. Egidio da Viterbo, "Address to the Fifth Lateran Council," in John C. Olin, *The Catholic Reformation*, 44-53, quote from 44.

24. Egidio da Viterbo, "Address to the Fifth Lateran Council," 51.

25. Egidio da Viterbo, "Address to the Fifth Lateran Council," 51.

26. Egidio da Viterbo, "Address to the Fifth Lateran Council," 52.

Chapter Three

1. Charles Odahl, *Constantine and the Christian Empire*, 2nd ed. (London: Routledge, 2004), 114–16.

2. Quoted in Charles Odahl, *Constantine and the Christian Empire*, 114.

3. Charles Odahl, *Constantine and the Christian Empire*, 113–14.

4. E. R. Chamberlin, *The Bad Popes* (New York: Dorset Press, 1969), 9.

5. Charles Odahl, *Constantine and the Christian Empire*, 115-16. See also, Noel Lenski, ed., *The Cambridge Companion to the Age of Constantine*, rev. ed. (Cambridge: Cambridge University Press, 2012), 282–95.

6. Friedrich Kempf, Hans-Georg Beck, Eugen Ewig, and Josef Jungmann, *The Church in the Age of Feudalism*, (New York: Herder and Herder, 1969), 23. This is Volume III of the series edited by Hubert Jedin and John Dolan, *Handbook of Church History*.

7. E. R. Chamberlin, *The Bad Popes* (New York: Dorset Press, 1969), 17.

8. For the term "republic of St. Peter," and an in-depth analysis of the origin and development of the Papal States,

see the above cited Thomas Noble, *The Republic of St. Peter*.

9. Thomas Noble, *The Republic of St. Peter*, 135. Noble has an extensive bibliography of the scholarly discussions.

10. Thomas Noble, *The Republic of St. Peter*, 136.

11. There is a convenient online version of the "Donation of Constantine" provided by Fordham University, available at http://sourcebooks.fordham.edu/source/donatconst.asp. I have used that version. See also the side by side, Latin and English version provided in Christopher Coleman, *The Treatise of Lorenzo Valla on the Donation of Constantine* (New Haven, CT: Yale University Press, 1922), 10–19.

12. Pope Gelasius I, On the Bond of Anathema, in in Brian Tierney, *The Crisis of Church & State* (Englewood Cliffs, NJ: Prentice-Hall, 1980), 14–15.

Chapter Four

1. Horace K. Mann, *The Lives of the Popes in the Early Middle Ages*, vol. IV (St. Louis: B. Herder, 1925), 34–35, and E. R. Chamberlin, *The Bad Popes* (New York: Dorset, 1969), 27, 289–90.

2. Horace K. Mann, *The Lives of the Popes in the Early Middle Ages*, vol. IV, 17.

3. Horace K. Mann, *The Lives of the Popes in the Early Middle Ages*, vol. IV, 17.

4. Horace K. Mann, *The Lives of the Popes in the Early Middle Ages*, vol. IV, 18.

5. Liudprand of Cremona, *Retribution*, II.48, in *The Complete Works of Liudprand of Cremona* (Washington, DC: Catholic University of America Press, 2007), translated by Paolo Squatriti.

6. Liudprand of Cremona, *Retribution*, II.48.

7. Liudprand asserts that Theodora forced herself sexually on John "over and over again." Liudprand of Cremona, *Retribution*, II.48.

8. Liudprand of Cremona, *Retribution*, II.48.

9. E. R. Chamberlin, *The Bad Popes*, 26.

10. Liudprand of Cremona, *Retribution*, III.43.

11. On Liudprand himself and scholarly assessments of his work see Paolo Squatriti's Introduction in *The Complete Works of Liudprand of Cremona*; Mann's discussion, Horace K. Mann, *The Lives of the Popes in the Early Middle Ages*, Vol. IV, 136–41; Friedrich Kempf, Hans-Georg Beck, Eugen Ewig, and Josef Jungmann, *The Church in the Age of Feudalism*, Vol. III of Hubert Jedin and John Dolan, eds., *Handbook of Church History* (New York, NY: Herder and Herder, 1969), 199; Thomas Noble and Julia Smith, eds., *Early Medieval Christianities, c. 600–c. 1100*, Vol. 3 of *The Cambridge History of Christianity* (Cambridge: Cambridge University Press, 2008), 221.

12. Liudprand of Cremona, *King Otto*, 20, in *The Complete Works of Liudprand of Cremona*.

13. Boniface VIII, *Unam Sanctam*, contained in Brian Tierney, *The Crisis of Church & State 1050–1300* (Englewood Cliffs, NJ: Prentice-Hall, 1964), 188–89.

14. Para, Heather, "Plague, Papacy and Power: The Effect of the Black Plague on the Avignon Papacy," *Saber and Scroll* (2016) Vol. 5: Issue 1, Article 3, 7–16, quote from 10.

15. Para, Heather, "Plague, Papacy and Power," 10.

16. Para, Heather, "Plague, Papacy and Power," 10.

17. Para, Heather, "Plague, Papacy and Power," 11.

18. Para, Heather, "Plague, Papacy and Power," 13–14.

19. Hans-Georg Beck, Karl Fink, Josef Glazik, Erwin Iserloh, and Hans Wolter, *From the High Middle Ages to the Eve of the Reformation*, Vol IV of Hubert Jedin and John Nolan, *History of the Church* (New York: Seabury, 1980), 531–32.

20. Hans-Georg Beck, Karl Fink, Josef Glazik, Erwin Iserloh, and Hans Wolter, *From the High Middle Ages to the Eve of the Reformation*, 543–44.

21. Eamon Duffy, *Saints and Sinners: A History of the Popes* (New Haven: Yale University Press, 2006, 3rd ed.), 191.

22. Eamon Duffy, *Saints and Sinners*, 194.

23. Ludwig Pastor, *The History of the Popes*, Vol V, *From the Close of the Middle Ages*, 5th ed. (St. Louis: Herder, 1950), 377.

24. Ludwig Pastor, *The History of the Popes*, Vol V, *From the Close of the Middle Ages*, 381–84.

25. Ludwig Pastor, *The History of the Popes*, Vol V, *From the Close of the Middle Ages*, 385.

26. Niccolò Machiavelli, *The Prince*, translated by Harvey Mansfield (Chicago: University of Chicago Press, 1985), XVIII, 70.

27. Niccolò Machiavelli, *The Prince*, XI, 46.

28. Scott Hahn and Benjamin Wiker, *Politicizing the Bible: the Roots of Historical Criticism and the Secularization of Scripture 1300–1700* (New York: Crossroad, 2013), 121.

29. Eamon Duffy, *Saints and Sinners*, 189.

30. Eamon Duffy, *Saints and Sinners*, 190.

31. Eamon Duffy, *Saints and Sinners*, 190.

32. Eamon Duffy, *Saints and Sinners*, 190.

33. See Richard Marius, *Martin Luther*, 79–83 and Martin Brecht, *Martin Luther: His Road to Reformation, 1483–1521*, translated by James Schaaf (Philadelphia: Fortress Press, 1985), 100–104.

Chapter Five

1. See David Wootton, "New Histories of Atheism" in Michael Hunter and David Wootton, eds., *Atheism from the Reformation to the Enlightenment* (Oxford: Clarendon Press, 1992), 13–53, names cited on p. 25. For additional background see also George Buckley, *Atheism in the English Renaissance* (Chicago: University of Chicago Press, 1932).

2. Epicurus, *Letter to Herodotus*, sections 38-44, in Brad Inwood and L. P. Gerson, *The Epicurus Reader* (Indianapolis: IN: Hackett, 1994).

3. Epicurus, *Letter to Herodotus*, section 67.

4. Epicurus, *Letter to Herodotus*, sections 76-77, 81; *Letter to Pythocles*, sections 113-116, likewise in Brad Inwood and L. P. Gerson, *The Epicurus Reader*.

5. Epicurus, *Letter to Menoeceus*, sections 124-125, in Brad Inwood and L. P. Gerson, *The Epicurus Reader*.

6. Epicurus, *Letter to Menoeceus*, sections 123–24.

7. Epicurus, *Letter to Menoeceus*, sections 128–32.

8. On the immense influence of Lucretius from the latter 1400s onward, see (along with the above-cited Peter Gay, *The Enlightenment*), Stuart Gillespie and Philip Hardie, eds., *The Cambridge Companion to Lucretius* (Cambridge: Cambridge University Press, 2007), chs. 8–9, 11-19; Alison Brown, *The Return of Lucretius to Renaissance Florence* (Cambridge, MA: Harvard, 2010).

9. Lucretius, *De Rerum Natura*, I, 62–65. My translation.

10. Lucretius, *De Rerum Natura*, I, 931–32.

11. Lucretius, *De Rerum Natura*, I, 78–79.

12. Lucretius, *De Rerum Natura*, I, 82–83.

13. The historian Peter Gay is especially good at tracing the Lucretian origins of modern unbelief. See his *The Enlightenment: an Interpretation. The Rise of Modern Paganism* (New York, NY: Norton, 1966), 98–105.

14. Lucretius, *De Rerum Natura*, III, 966–1023.

15. See the entire of Book V, especially V, 416–31, 771–877. On the widespread presence of evolutionary theory before Charles Darwin see my *Darwin Myth* (Washington, DC: Regnery, 2009).

16. Lucian, *The Lover of Lies*, 32, 37.

17. Lucian, *The Passing of Peregrinus*, 11, translated by A. M. Harmon in *Lucian* (Cambridge: Harvard University Press, 1962), vol. V.

18. Lucian, *The Passing of Peregrinus*, 12–13.

19. Lucian, *The Passing of Peregrinus*, 13.

20. Livy, I, xix, 4-5. My translation.

21. Plutarch, *Parallel Lives*, Numa, iv.7–8. My translation.

22. Polybius, *Histories*, VI, 56.6–13. My translation.

23. See Averroës, *The Book of the Decisive Treatise, Determining the Connection between the Law and Wisdom*, translated by Charles Butterworth (Provo, Utah: Brigham Young University Press, 2001), ch. III and *Averroes' Tahafut Al-Tahafut*, Volumes I and III, translated by Simon Van Den Bergh (Cambridge: Cambridge University Press, 1987): 580–88 ("About the Natural Sciences," Fourth Discussion, 359–63).

24. Nicholas Davidson, "Unbelief and Atheism in Italy, 1500–1700," in Michael Hunter and David Wootton, eds., *Atheism from the Reformation to the Enlightenment*, 55–85. Quote from 59.

25. For the difficulties in sorting things out, see David Wootton, "New Histories of Atheism."

26. Nicholas Davidson, "Unbelief and Atheism in Italy, 1500–1700," in Michael Hunter and David Wootton, eds., *Atheism from the Reformation to the Enlightenment*, 55–85. Quote from 55.

27. Quoted in Nicholas Davidson, "Unbelief and Atheism in Italy, 1500–1700," 55–56.

28. David Wootton has offered a skeptical account of the sincerity of Galileo's faith in his *Galileo: Watcher of the Skies* (New Haven, CT: Yale University Press, 2010), esp. 240–50.

29. Nicholas Davidson, "Unbelief and Atheism in Italy, 1500–1700," 56.

30. Happily, the Council's proceedings are available online: http://www.papalencyclicals.net/Councils/ecum18.htm.

31. Nicholas Davidson, "Unbelief and Atheism in Italy, 1500–1700," 56.

32. See Nicholas Davidson, "Unbelief and Atheism in Italy, 1500–1700," 65–67.

Chapter Six
1. See the Koran, 2.53, 2.87, 5.44, 5.46, 29.46.

2. Koran, 3.35–59, 19.1–34.

3. Koran 3.45–47, 3.59, 19.16–22.

4. Koran, 4.171, 61.6–7.

5. Koran 3:48–51.

6. Koran 4.156–158.

7. Koran 43.59–61.

8. Koran, 19.34–35, 23.91, 4.171, 5.72–75, 5.116.

9. Koran 2.88–89, 2.97–99, 2.101, 3.3–4, 3.12, 4.48.

10. It's nearly impossible for most people either to find or wade through the volumes upon volumes of the *Hadiths*. Happily, the Center for Muslim-Jewish Engagement has put the

Hadiths on the Internet in a searchable format. See http://www.cmje.org/. I'll use the CMJE's version for that reason.

11.   So, for example, today we witness members of ISIS stoning adulteresses. The punishment for adultery in the Koran is actually "a hundred lashes" (Koran, 24.2). But according to the *Hadiths*, Muhammad himself directed an adulterer to be stoned. While some Muslims reject the stoning of adulterers, since it is not found in the Koran, most affirm the authority of the *Hadiths*. Thus, the objection that the penalty for stoning is not in the Koran holds no weight for most Muslims. In fact, the *Hadiths* specifically both foresee this objection and reject it, thereby affirming stoning as the penalty for adultery. *Volume 7, Book 63, Number 196,* and *Volume 8, Book 82, Number 816,* available at http://www.usc.edu/org/cmje/religious-texts/hadith/bukhari/063-sbt.php#007.063.196, and http://www.usc.edu/org/cmje/religious-texts/hadith/bukhari/082-sbt.php#008.082.816.

12.   See the discussion of such attempts along with rebuttals in Andrew G. Bostom, ed., *The Legacy of Jihad: Islamic Holy War and the Fate of Non-Muslims* (Amherst, NY: Prometheus Books, 2008).

13.   Koran, 9.29. See also 9.5, 9.73, 9.111, 9.123, 4.74, 4.76, 4.95, 2.216–218, 2.191, 8.12, 8.15–16, 8.39, 8.41, 8.65, 48.20. Readers will want to consult various translations, the translation given above being a kind of amalgam of several consulted.

14.   http://www.usc.edu/org/cmje/religious-texts/hadith/muslim/019-smt.php#019.4294.

15. http://www.usc.edu/org/cmje/religious-texts/hadith/ bukhari/052-sbt.php.

16. *Volume 4, Book 52, Number 196*. Available at http://www. usc.edu/org/cmje/religious-texts/hadith/bukhari/052-sbt. php.

17. For more detail see Andrew G. Bostom, ed., *The Legacy of Jihad*, ch. 1.

18. Koran, 8.39.

19. Koran, 8.55.

20. Koran, 8.65.

21. See the detailed, century-by-century account of continual wars of jihad from the 600s to the 1500s in Andrew G. Bostom, ed., *The Legacy of Jihad*, 589–627.

22. Serge Trifkovic, *The Sword of the Prophet* (Boston: Regina Orthodox Press, 2002), 95–96.

23. Efraim Karsh, *Islamic Imperialism: A History* (New Haven, CT: Yale University Press, 2007), 60–61.

24. Andrew G. Bostom, ed., *The Legacy of Jihad*, 48–49.

25. Andrew G. Bostom, ed., *The Legacy of Jihad*, 49–50.

26. Efraim Karsh, *Islamic Imperialism*, 76.

27. Efraim Karsh, *Islamic Imperialism*, 76–77.

28. Efraim Karsh, *Islamic Imperialism*, 77.

29. Efraim Karsh, *Islamic Imperialism*, 91.

30. Efraim Karsh, *Islamic Imperialism*, 93.

31. Efraim Karsh, *Islamic Imperialism*, 93.

32. Efraim Karsh, *Islamic Imperialism*, 93.

33. Quoted in Sarah Henrich and James L. Boyce, "Martin Luther—Translations of Two Prefaces on Islam: *Preface to the Libellus de ritu et moribus Turcorum* (1530), and *Preface to Bibliander's Edition of the Qur'an* (1543)," *Word & World*, Vol XVI, No 2, Spring 1996, 250–66, quote from 252.

34. Sarah Henrich and James L. Boyce, "Martin Luther—Translations of Two Prefaces on Islam," 252.

35. Quoted in Sarah Henrich and James L. Boyce, "Martin Luther—Translations of Two Prefaces on Islam," 253.

36. Quoted in Sarah Henrich and James L. Boyce, "Martin Luther—Translations of Two Prefaces on Islam," 254.

37. Quoted in Sarah Henrich and James L. Boyce, "Martin Luther—Translations of Two Prefaces on Islam," 255.

38. Quoted in Sarah Henrich and James L. Boyce, "Martin Luther—Translations of Two Prefaces on Islam," 259.

39. Sarah Henrich and James L. Boyce, "Martin Luther—Translations of Two Prefaces on Islam," 255.

40. Quoted in Sarah Henrich and James L. Boyce, "Martin Luther—Translations of Two Prefaces on Islam," 263.

41. He begins the preface to the Koran with the following words: "Many persons have authored small tracts describing the rites, beliefs, and customs of Jews of this day for the very purpose of more easily refuting their manifest lies and exposed errors and ravings. There is no doubt that, when pious minds bring the testimony of the prophets to bear on the delusions and blasphemies of those people, they are greatly confirmed in faith and in love for the truth of the

gospel and are fired with a righteous hatred of the perversity of the Jewish teachings. Indeed let any sane or moderate person consider how much of the most tasteless slander, how much madness and wickedness there is in Jewish beliefs and rites…" Quoted in Sarah Henrich and James L. Boyce, "Martin Luther—Translations of Two Prefaces on Islam," 262.

42. The Jews were an especial target for Muhammad since they resisted his demands to convert, as well as rejected his claims to be a prophet. The animosity against Jews lasts until the end of time. In the Koran, Allah threatens to turn them into apes, pigs, and slaves. See Koran 5.60, and also in general, 2.88, 2.98, 3.67, 4.46–50, 4.461, 5.13, 5.33, 5.41, 5.51, 5.64. After gaining full control over Medina, Muhammad took revenge on his detractors, including poets who had written verses critical of him, the first being a woman, Asma bint Marwan, whom he ordered slain. One of the next was a Jewish poet, Ka'b bin al-Ashraf, whom he had beheaded. He then instructed his followers to kill any Jew whom they met, the first victim being a Jewish merchant, Ibn Sunayna. His followers then killed an elderly Jewish merchant Abu Rafi—again, Muhammad heartily approved. Next, Muhammad attacked the Jewish Banu Nadir tribe, then the Jewish Banu-'l-Mustaliq tribe (raping the women), and the Banu Qurayza tribe was attacked in 627AD (about nine hundred males were beheaded in front of their women and children, after they refused to convert, and then the women were raped), and the Jews at Khaybar in 628. Thus, Muhammad engaged in a kind of ethnic cleansing of the Jews by Muslims. On this successive

"cleansing" see Serge Trifkovic, *The Sword of the Prophet* (Boston: Regina Orthodox Press, 2002), 40–44. The slaughter of the Banu Qurayza tribe is celebrated in the Koran, 33.25–26.

43. Quoted in Sarah Henrich and James L. Boyce, "Martin Luther—Translations of Two Prefaces on Islam," 266.

44. Emidio Campi, "Early Reformed Attitudes towards Islam," *Theological Review* 31 (2010),131–51; material on Bullinger, 143–44.

45. Emidio Campi, "Early Reformed Attitudes towards Islam," 146–50.

46. Jan Slomp, "Calvin and the Turks," *Studies in Interreligious Dialogue* 19 (2009), 50–65; quote from 52.

47. Quoted in Jan Slomp, "Calvin and the Turks," 56.

48. Quoted in Jan Slomp, "Calvin and the Turks," 57.

49. Jan Slomp, "Calvin and the Turks," 52.

50. Jan Slomp, "Calvin and the Turks," 53.

51. Jonathan Israel, *Enlightenment Contested: Philosophy, Modernity, and the Emancipation of Man, 1670–1752* (Oxford: Oxford University Press, 2006), 616.

52. These would include the French philosopher Pierre Bayle (1647–1706), French historian Henri de Boulainvilliers (1658–1722), the Irish freethinker John Toland (1670–1722), the Italian freethinker Alberto Radicati (1698–1737), the freethinking Huguenot Jean-Frédéric Bernard (1683–1744), the French materialist Nicholas Fréret (1688–1749), the French philosopher Jean-Baptiste de Boyer, Marquis d'Argens (1704–1771), Jean-Jacques Rousseau (1712–1778),

and even the greatest and loudest of the Enlightenment *philosophes*, the great enemy of Christianity, the Frenchman Voltaire (1694–1778).

53. Jonathan Israel, *Enlightenment Contested*, 619.

54. Jonathan Israel, *Enlightenment Contested*, 620.

55. Jonathan Israel, *Enlightenment Contested*, 620–39.

Chapter Seven

1. Eamon Duffy, *Saints & Sinners*, 194.

2. Quoted in Joseph Strayer, *Medieval Statecraft and the Perspectives of History* (Princeton: Princeton University Press, 1971), 313.

3. Michael Wilks, "Royal Patronage and Anti-Papalism from Ockham to Wyclif," in Anne Hudson and Michael Wilks, *From Ockham to Wyclif* (Oxford: Basil Blackwell, 1987), 135–63. Quote from 151.

4. J. W. McKenna, "How God became an Englishman," *Tudor Rule and Revolution: Essays for G. R. Elton*, ed. D. J. Guth and J. W. McKenna (Cambridge, 1982), 25–43

5. Gerald Bray, ed., *Documents of the English Reformation* (Minneapolis, MN: Fortress Press, 1994), 113–14.

6. Bob Scribner, Roy Porter, and Mikuláš Teich, *The Reformation in National Context* (Cambridge: Cambridge University Press, 1994), 6.

7. The Archbishop's letter, along with the context, can be found in Gerald Strauss, *Manifestations of Discontent in*

Germany on the Eve of the Reformation (Bloomington: Indiana University Press, 1971), 37–40.

8. Bob Scribner, Roy Porter, and Mikuláš Teich, *The Reformation in National Context*, 10.

9. Quoted in A. G. Dickens, *The German Nation and Martin Luther*, 38–39. For an excellent general account of these developments, see W. Bradford Smith, "Germanic Pagan Antiquity in Lutheran Historical Thought," *Journal of the Historical Society* IV:3 (2004), 351–74.

10. See Donald Kelley, "*Tacitus Noster*: the *Germania* in the Renaissance and Reformation," in T. J. Luce and A. J. Woodman, eds., *Tacitus and the Tacitean Tradition* (Princeton, NJ: Princeton University Press, 1993), ch. 8.

11. Gerald Strauss, *Manifestations of Discontent in Germany on the Eve of the Reformation*, 75–82; Hajo Holborn, *Ulrich von Hutten and the German Reformation*, 74–76.

12. See A. G. Dickens, *The German Nation and Martin Luther* (London: Edward Arnold, 1974), pp. 8-16; Norman Cohn, *The Pursuit of the Millennium: Revolutionary Millenarians and Mystical Anarchists of the Middle Ages*, rev. ed. (New York: Oxford University Press, 1970), 118–26.

13. Michael Wilks, "Royal Patronage and Anti-Papalism from Ockham to Wyclif," in Anne Hudson and Michael Wilks, *From Ockham to Wyclif* (Oxford: Basil Blackwell, 1987), 135–63. Quote from 152.

Chapter Eight

1. For a much more detailed account of Marsilius and his thought, with ample bibliography, see Scott Hahn and Benjamin Wiker, *Politicizing the Bible: The Roots of Historical Criticism and the Secularization of Scripture 1300–1700* (New York, NY: Crossroad, 2013), ch. 2.

2. Étienne Gilson, *History of Christian Philosophy in the Middle Ages* (New York: Random House, 1955), 526.

3. Marsilius of Padua, *Defensor Pacis*, translated by Alan Gewirth (Toronto, Canada: University of Toronto Press, 1980), I, 5.11.

4. Marsilius of Padua, *Defensor Pacis*, I, 9.2.

5. Marsilius of Padua, *Defensor Pacis*, I, 28.1; II, 19.1. While this might sound pious, Marsilius then establishes the irrationality of Christian faith precisely *because* it has no other foundation than Scripture. As Marsilius remarked with a barely suppressed smirk, believers must first accept the Bible itself as true in order to accept what it reveals, for its truth is "proved only by the authorities of these Scriptures themselves..." Marsilius of Padua, *Defensor Pacis*, II, 19.1–3, 10. In Marsilius' mind, that is circular reasoning, and hence no reasoning at all. And so, to him, Christianity seemed no more firmly based than Islam, thereby reaffirming that Averroes' philosophical approach was the right one to take.

6. Marsilius of Padua, *Defensor Pacis*, II, 19.3.

7. To quote from Marsilius, "Hence in the twenty-second chapter of Matthew and the eleventh of Mark: 'Render unto Caesar the things that are Caesar's,' by 'Caesar'

signifying any rule. So too the Apostle said in the thirteenth chapter of Romans, and it bears repeating: 'Let every soul be subject to the higher powers.' So too in the first epistle to Timothy, last chapter: 'Even to infidel lords,' ...From all these it is quite evident that Christ, the Apostle, and the saints held the view that all men must be subject to the human laws and to the judges according to these laws." Marsilius of Padua, *Defensor Pacis*, II, 9.9.

8. Marsilius of Padua, *Defensor Pacis*, II, 9.9.

9. Marsilius of Padua, *Defensor Pacis*, II, 2, throughout.

10. Marsilius of Padua, *Defensor Pacis*, II.11.4.

11. Niccolò Machiavelli, *Discourses on Livy*, translated by Harvey Mansfield and Nathan Tarcov (Chicago: University of Chicago Press, 1996), I.11.1–3.

12. Machiavelli, *Discourses on Livy*, I.12.1.

13. Niccolò Machiavelli, *The Prince*, translated by Harvey Mansfield (Chicago: University of Chicago Press, 1985), XVIII, 70.

14. Niccolò Machiavelli, *The Prince*, XV, 61.

15. J. W. McKenna, "How God became an Englishman," 27.

16. J. W. McKenna, "How God became an Englishman," 29–30.

17. Michael Wilks, "Royal Patronage and Anti-Papalism from Ockham to Wyclif," 147–48. I have "corrected" the spelling in Wilks' quote, who uses another of the multiple spellings of Wycliffe.

18. See G. R. Evans, *John Wyclif: Myth & Reality* (Downers Grove, IL: InterVarsity Press, 2005), 164–65 and Margaret

Harvey, "Adam Easton and the Condemnation of John Wyclif," *English Historical Review* 118 (1998), 321–34.

19. Edith C. Tatnall, "John Wyclif and *Ecclesia Anglicana,*" *Journal of Ecclesiastical History*, Vol. 20, No. 1, April 1969, 19–43. Quote from 34. Again, spelling made uniform.

20. Michael Wilks, "Royal Patronage and Anti-Papalism from Ockham to Wyclif," 157–58.

21. W. Gordon Zeeveld, *Foundations of Tudor Policy* (London: Methuen & Co., Ltd., 1969), 14, 37–38, 46, 113, 184–89; Felix Raab, *The English Face of Machiavelli* (London: Routledge & Kegan Paul, 1964), esp. 31–38, ; Peter Donaldson, *Machiavelli and Mystery of State* (Cambridge: Cambridge University Press, 1988), 32; Paul O'Grady, *Henry VIII and the Conforming Catholics* (Collegeville, MN: The Liturgical Press, 1990), Ch. 3; Scott Hahn and Benjamin Wiker, *Politicizing the Bible*, Ch. 6, especially 236–45; Harry S. Stout, "Marsilius of Padua and the Henrician Reformation," *Church History* (1974) 43, 308–18; J. Patrick Coby, *Thomas Cromwell: Machiavellian Statecraft and the English Reformation* (Lanham, MD: Lexington Books, 2009).

22. W. Gordon Zeeveld, *Foundations of Tudor Policy*, 133–35.

23. Victoria Kahn, *Machiavellian Rhetoric from the Counter-Reformation to Milton* (Princeton: Princeton University Press, 1994), 136; Peter Donaldson, *Machiavelli and Mystery of State*, 32.

24. Felix Raab, *The English Face of Machiavelli*, 31; W. Gordon Zeeveld, *Foundations of Tudor Policy*, 14.

25. For those interested in Henry VIII's brutal, Marsilian and Machiavellian actions and policies see J. J. Scarisbrick, *Henry VIII* (Berkeley and Los Angeles: University of California Press, 1968); John Matusiak, *Henry VIII: the Life and Rule of England's Nero* (Gloucestershire, UK: History Press, 2013); and Scott Hahn and Benjamin Wiker, *Politicizing the Bible*, ch. 6.

26. For the spread of Machiavelli's teachings in areas other than England, and the consequent ambiguity, see Keith Howard, *The Reception of Machiavelli in Early Modern Spain* (Suffolk, UK: Tamesis, 2014); the above-cited E. A. Rees, *Political Thought from Machiavelli to Stalin*; and Friedrich Meinecke, *Machiavellism: The Doctrine of Raison d'Etat and Its Place in Modern History*, translated by Douglas Scott (London: Routledge, 1957).

Chapter Nine

1. The following are all very helpful accounts of Luther's life and thought: Martin Brecht, *Martin Luther: His Road to Reformation, 1483–1521*, translated by James Schaaf (Philadelphia, PA: Fortress Press, 1985); and Heiko Oberman, *Luther: Man between God and the Devil*, translated by Eileen Walliser-Schwarzbart (New Haven: Yale University Press, 1989). For general background, see R. W. Scribner and C. Scott Dixon, *The German Reformation*, second ed. (New York: Palgrave Macmillan, 2003).

2. See Richard Marius, *Martin Luther*, 44–45 and Martin Brecht, *Martin Luther: His Road to Reformation, 1483–1521*, 48–49.

3. Heiko Oberman, *Luther: Man between God and the Devil*, 146–50.

4. Martin Luther, "Preface to the Complete Edition of Luther's Latin Writings," contained in John Dillenberger, ed., *Martin Luther: Selections from His Writings* (New York: Doubleday, 1961), 10–11.

5. See Richard Marius, *Martin Luther: the Christian between God and Death* (Cambridge, Massachusetts: Belknap Press, 1999), 137–38.

6. The ninety-five theses are contained in John Dillenberger, ed., *Martin Luther: Selections from His Writings*, (New York: Doubleday, 1961), 489–500.

7. Reform of indulgences did indeed come, but too late, at the Council of Trent in 1546: "the sacred holy Synod teaches, and enjoins, that the use of Indulgences, for the Christian people most salutary, and approved of by the authority of sacred Councils, is to be retained in the Church...[but] It desires that...the abuses which have crept therein, and by occasion of which this honorable name of Indulgences is blasphemed by heretics, be amended and corrected, It ordains generally by this decree, that all evil gains for the obtaining thereof,-whence a most prolific cause of abuses amongst the Christian people has been derived,-be wholly abolished." Session. 25, *Decree on Indulgences*, helpfully available at http://www.thecounciloftrent.com/ch25.htm.

8. Diarmaid MacCulloch, *The Reformation: A History*, 121.

9. Quoted in Richard Marius, *Martin Luther: the Christian between God and Death*, 282–83.

10. Quoted in (among many places) Richard Marius, *Martin Luther: the Christian between God and Death*, p. 294. The famous rhetorical flourish, "Here I stand; I can do no other," was added in a later printed version at Wittenberg.

11. All quotes from Martin Luther, *An Appeal to the Ruling Class of German Nationality as to the Amelioration of the State of Christendom* in John Dillenberger, ed., *Martin Luther: Selections from His Writings*, 403–85; quote from 406.

12. Martin Luther, *An Appeal to the Ruling Class of German Nationality*, 406–7.

13. Martin Luther, *An Appeal to the Ruling Class of German Nationality*, 408–9.

14. Martin Luther, *An Appeal to the Ruling Class of German Nationality*, 414–15.

15. Martin Luther, *An Appeal to the Ruling Class of German Nationality*, 415.

16. See John Oyer, *Lutheran Reformers against Anabaptists* (Hague: Martinus Nijhoff, 1964), 9–12, 24–27; Susan Karant-Nunn, *Zwickau in Transition, 1500–1547* (Columbus, OH: Ohio State University Press, 1987), 104; Ronald Sider, *Andreas Bodenstein von Karlstadt: the Development of His Thought, 1517–1525* (Leiden: E. J. Brill, 1974), 110; David Steinmetz, *Reformers in the Wings: From Geiler von Kayserberg to Theodore Beza*, second ed. (Oxford: Oxford University Press, 2001), 127–29; Diarmaid MacCulloch, *The Reformation*, 137–57 .

17. Diarmaid MacCulloch, *The Reformation*, 143.

18. Richard Marius, *Martin Luther: the Christian between God and Death* (Cambridge, Massachusetts: Belknap Press, 1999), 325; Mark Edwards, *Luther and the False Brethren* (Stanford, CA: Stanford University Press, 1975), 22–23.

19. This quote comes from Luther's *Against the Heavenly Prophets in the Matter of Images and Sacraments* contained in Ronald Sider, *Karlstadt's Battle with Luther: documents in a Liberal-Radical Debate* (Philadelphia, PA: Fortress Press, 1978), 94.

20. Diarmaid MacCulloch, *The Reformation*, 146.

21. Diarmaid MacCulloch, *The Reformation*, 148.

22. Diarmaid MacCulloch, *The Reformation*, 150.

23. See the useful discussion on the difficulty of sorting out the Anabaptists in Carlos Eire, *Reformations: The Early Modern World, 1450–1650* (New Haven, CT: Yale University Press, 2016), ch. 11.

24. For a general account, see Lee Wandel, *Voracious Idols and Violent Hands: Iconoclasm in Reformation Zurich, Strasbourg, and Basel* (Cambridge: Cambridge University Press, 1995). Luther's position on images and the outbreak of iconoclasm see Tarald Rasmussen, "Iconoclasm and Religious Images in the Early Lutheran Tradition," in Kristine Kolrud and Marina Prusac, *Iconoclasm from Antiquity to Modernity* (Burlington, VT: Ashgate, 2014), Ch. 7, 107–18.

25. Diarmaid MacCulloch, *The Reformation*, 155–56.

26. See Phyllis Crew, *Calvinist preaching and iconoclasm in the Netherlands, 1544–1569* (Cambridge: Cambridge

University Press, 1978); and Andrew Spicer, "Iconoclasm on the Frontier: Le Cateau-Cambrésis, 1566), in Kristine Kolrud and Marina Prusac, *Iconoclasm from Antiquity to Modernity*, Ch. 8, 119–37.

27. Diarmaid MacCulloch, *The Reformation*, 158.

28. Quoted in Richard Marius, *Martin Luther*, 431.

29. Quoted in Richard Marius, *Martin Luther*, 432–33.

30. Richard Marius, *Martin Luther*, 434–35.

31. Martin Luther, *Commentary on Psalm 82*, 62–63. Duncan Forrester, "Martin Luther and John Calvin," 317.

32. W. D. J. Cargill Thompson, *The Political Thought of Martin Luther*, 24–25.

33. On this whole embarrassing affair see Hastings Eells, *The Attitude of Martin Bucer toward the Bigamy of Philip of Hesse* (New Haven, CT: Yale University Press, 1924); Martin Brecht, *Martin Luther: The Preservation of the Church, 1532–1546*, translated by James Schaaf (Minneapolis, MN: Fortress Press, 1993), 205–15; Scott Hahn and Benjamin Wiker, *Politicizing the Bible*, 180–83.

Chapter Ten

1. You can add to that the development of paper and the paper-making industry. See Lucien Febvre and Henry-Jean Martin, *The Coming of the Book: The Impact of Printing 1450–1800*, translated by David Gerard (London: Verso, 1997), 29–44.

2. Elizabeth Eisenstein, *The Printing Press as an Agent of Change: Communications and Cultural Transformations in*

Early-Modern Europe (Cambridge: Cambridge University Press, 1979), 303.

3. See David O. Frantz, "'Leud Priapians' and Renaissance Pornography," *Studies in English Literature, 1500–1900*, vol. 12, No. 1, The English Renaissance (Winter, 1972), 157–72, esp. 165–66. Also: Lynn Hunt, ed. *The Invention of Pornography: Obscenity and the Origins of Modernity, 1500–1800* (New York: Zone Books, 1993); James Turner, *Libertines and Radicals in Early Modern London: Sexuality, Politics, and Literary Culture, 1630-1685* (Cambridge: Cambridge University Press, 2002); and Saad El-Gabalawy, "Aretino's Pornography and Renaissance Satire," *Rocky Mountain Review* Vol. 30, No. 2 (Spring, 1976), 87–99.

4. Lucien Febvre and Henry-Jean Martin, *The Coming of the Book*, 244–45.

5. Lucien Febvre and Henry-Jean Martin, *The Coming of the Book*, 245–46.

6. Lucien Febvre and Henry-Jean Martin, *The Coming of the Book*, 246–47.

7. Elizabeth Eisenstein, *The Printing Press as an Agent of Change*, 307–8, and footnotes 17–18.

8. Quoted in Elizabeth Eisenstein, *The Printing Press as an Agent of Change*, 306–7.

9. Diarmaid MacCulloch, *The Reformation*, 152. For a summary of the volume of printing, its sources, and other interesting aspects of the flurry of printing around Luther, see Mark Edwards, *Printing, Propaganda, and Martin Luther* (Berkeley, CA: University of California Press, 1994),

ch. 1. On Wittenberg as a major center of printing see Andrew Pettegree, *The Book in the Renaissance* (New Haven, CT: Yale, 2010), ch. 5.

10. Elizabeth Eisenstein, *The Printing Press as an Agent of Change*, 375.

11. Elizabeth Eisenstein, *The Printing Press as an Agent of Change*, 375–76.

12. Elizabeth Eisenstein, *The Printing Press as an Agent of Change*, 377.

13. On the economic aspects of printing see Andrew Pettegree, *The Book in the Renaissance*, 65–90.

14. Mark Edwards, *Printing, Propaganda, and Martin Luther*, 15.

15. Mark Edwards, *Printing, Propaganda, and Martin Luther*, 26; on Luther's assessment of Müntzer see Diarmaid MacCulloch, *The Reformation*, 161.

16. Quoted in Carter Lindberg, *The European Reformations*, second ed. (West Sussex, UK: John Wiley & Sons, 2010), 145, 147.

17. Mark Edwards, *Printing, Propaganda, and Martin Luther*, 29.

18. On the enormous effects Calvin had through printing and on printing, especially in Geneva, see Andrew Pettegree, *The Book in the Renaissance*, 207–11.

19. Elizabeth Eisenstein, *The Printing Press as an Agent of Change*, 345–46.

20. Elizabeth Eisenstein, *The Printing Press as an Agent of Change*, 363.

21. Elizabeth Eisenstein, *The Printing Press as an Agent of Change*, 371.

22. Mark Edwards, *Printing, Propaganda, and Martin Luther* (Berkeley, CA: University of California Press, 1994), 12.

23. Luther's Preface to the New Testament is contained in John Dillenberger, ed., *Martin Luther: Selections from His Writings*, 14–18. Quote from 14.

24. Contained in John Dillenberger, ed., *Martin Luther: Selections from His Writings*, 18–19. Emphasis added.

25. Quoted in Ronald Sider, Ronald Sider, *Andreas Bodenstein von Karlstadt: The Development of His Thought, 1517–1525* (Leiden: E. J. Brill, 1974), 97.

26. See Mark Edwards, *Printing, Propaganda, and Martin Luther*, 118–23.

27. See Mark Edwards, *Printing, Propaganda, and Martin Luther*, 129.

28. Mark Edwards, *Printing, Propaganda, and Martin Luther*, 143.

29. Mark Edwards, *Printing, Propaganda, and Martin Luther*, 144–45.

30. Council of Trent, Fourth Session, April, 1546, in Rev. H. J. Schroeder, O.P., *Canons and Decrees of the Council of Trent* (Rockford, IL: Tan, 1987), 17–20.

31. For an overview see Robert E. McNally, S.J., "The Council of Trent and Vernacular Bibles," *Theological Studies*, Vol. 27, No. 2. (June 1966), 204–27.

32. Quoted in Robert E. McNally, S.J., "The Council of Trent and Vernacular Bibles," 227.

33. See Desiderius Erasmus, *The Praise of Folly and Other Writings*, edited and translated by Robert Adams (New York, NY: Norton, 1989), 134.

34. Quoted in John Olin, *Catholic Reform: from Cardinal Ximenes to the Council of Trent, 1495–1563* (New York, NY: Fordham University Press, 1990), "Cardinal Ximenes' Dedicatory Prologue to the Complutensian Polyglot Bible 1517," 61–64. Quote from 62.

35. Quoted in John Olin, *Catholic Reform*, 64.

Chapter Eleven

1. See the entire of Scott Hahn and Benjamin Wiker, *Politicizing the Bible*, cited previously.

2. Scott Hahn and Benjamin Wiker, *Politicizing the Bible*, 131–42; Machiavelli, *The Prince*, VI; Machiavelli, *Discourses on Livy*, I.9.1–3, I.11.1–3, III.30.1.

3. Again, see Scott Hahn and Benjamin Wiker, *Politicizing the Bible*, 265–66.

4. Richard Popkin, "Cartesianism and Biblical Criticism," 61.

5. On Hobbes' atheism, and the unsuccessful attempts by some scholars to deny it, see Scott Hahn and Benjamin Wiker, *Politicizing the Bible*, 285–96, with extensive bibliography.

6. For a smattering of such attributions, see see Jon D. Levenson, *The Hebrew Bible, the Old Testament, and Historical Criticism: Jews and Christians in Biblical Studies* (Louisville: Westminster/John Knox Press, 1993), 95 and 117; John H. Hayes, "The History of the Study of

Israelite and Judaean History," in John H. Hayes and J. Maxwell Miller (eds.), *Israelite and Judaean History* (London: SCM Press, 1977), 45; J. Samuel Preus, "The Bible and Religion in the Century of Genius: Part II: The Rise and Fall of the Bible," *Religion*, 28 (1998), 22; Joseph Blenkinsopp, *The Pentateuch: An Introduction to the First Five Books of the Bible* (New York: Doubleday, 1992), 2; James Barr, "Interpretation, History of Modern Biblical Criticism," in Bruce M. Metzger and Michael D. Coogan (eds.), *The Oxford Companion to the Bible* (Oxford: Oxford University Press, 1993), 322; Richard Popkin, "Bible Criticism and Social Science," in Robert S. Cohen and Marx W. Wartofsky (eds.), *Methodological and Historical Essays in the Natural and Social Sciences* (Dordrecht: D. Reidel Publishing, 1974), 339.

7. See Elizabeth Haldane and G. R. T. Ross, translators, *The Philosophical Works of Descartes* (New York: Dover, 1955), Vol. II, Objection III.ii, 61–62.

8. Thomas Hobbes, *Leviathan*, IV.34 and 46.

9. See his "natural" explanation for religion in the *Leviathan*, I.11–12.

10. Hobbes, *Leviathan*, III.34.

11. Hobbes, *Leviathan*, II.26, 31; III.33, 42.

12. See Scott Hahn and Benjamin Wiker, *Politicizing the Bible*, 315–24.

13. Descartes, *Discourse on Method*, III.31.

14. On this honorary title, see Travis Frampton, *Spinoza and the Rise of Historical Criticism of the Bible* (London: T & T Clark, 2006), Introduction.

15. For a more thorough analysis, with ample bibliography, see Scott Hahn and Benjamin Wiker, *Politicizing the Bible*, ch. 9; the entire of Jonathan Israel, *Radical Enlightenment: Philosophy and the Making of Modernity 1650-1750* (Oxford: Oxford University Press, 2001).

16. Benedict Spinoza, *Ethics,* I, Def. 6; I, Props. 7, 11, 14, 18, 29 (Scholium), 33. There is a useful translation by Samuel Shirley included in Baruch Spinoza, *Ethics; Treatise on the Emendation of the Intellect; and Selected Letters* (Indianapolis, IN: Hackett Publishing, 1992).

17. On Spinoza's set of deductions and conclusions see Scott Hahn and Benjamin Wiker, *Politicizing the Bible*, 364–68.

18. For an excellent edition, see Benedict Spinoza, *Theologico-Political Treatise*, translated by Martin Yaffe (Newburyport, MA: R. Pullins & Company, 2004).

19. Benedict Spinoza, *Theologico-Political Treatise*, 2.8.5; 6.1.56–59, 73, 76, 80–85.

20. Benedict Spinoza, *Theologico-Political Treatise*, 6.1.67.

21. Benedict Spinoza, *Theologico-Political Treatise*, 13.1.2–4.

22. Benedict Spinoza, *Theologico-Political Treatise*, 12.2.45; 13.1.9–10.

23. See Scott Hahn and Benjamin Wiker, *Politicizing the Bible*, 368–93.

Chapter Twelve

1. S. H. Steinberg, *The 'Thirty Years War,' and the Conflict for European Hegemony 1600–1660* (London: Edward Arnold Publishers, 1966), 19–22.

2. Richard Dunn, *The Age of Religious Wars, 1559–1715*, 2nd ed. (New York: Norton, 1979), 60.

3. Richard Dunn, *The Age of Religious Wars, 1559–1715*, 60.

4. S. H. Steinberg, *The 'Thirty Years War,' and the Conflict for European Hegemony 1600–1660*, 24–25.

5. S. H. Steinberg, *The 'Thirty Years War,' and the Conflict for European Hegemony 1600–1660*, 30–31.

6. Richard Dunn, *The Age of Religious Wars, 1559–1715*, 80.

7. S. H. Steinberg, *The 'Thirty Years War,' and the Conflict for European Hegemony 1600–1660*, 38.

8. S. H. Steinberg, *The 'Thirty Years War,' and the Conflict for European Hegemony 1600–1660*, 38.

9. Richard Dunn, *The Age of Religious Wars, 1559–1715*, 84.

10. Richard Bonney, *The Thirty Years' War, 1618–1648* (Oxford: Osprey Publishing, 2002), 26.

11. Richard Bonney, *The Thirty Years' War, 1618–1648*, 33–34.

12. Richard Bonney, *The Thirty Years' War, 1618–1648*, 71.

13. Richard Dunn, *The Age of Religious Wars, 1559–1715*, 85.

14. Richard Dunn, *The Age of Religious Wars, 1559–1715*, 86.

15. Richard Dunn, *The Age of Religious Wars, 1559–1715*, 87.

16. S. H. Steinberg, *The 'Thirty Years War,' and the Conflict for European Hegemony 1600–1660*, 54.

17. Richard Dunn, *The Age of Religious Wars, 1559–1715*, 89.

18. S. H. Steinberg, *The 'Thirty Years War,' and the Conflict for European Hegemony 1600–1660*, 13–14.

19. On the spread of Machiavelli's ideas in regard to reason of state, see Friedrich Meinecke, *Machiavellianism: the Doctrine of Raison d'Etat and Its Place in Modern History*, translated by Douglas Scott (New York: Frederick A. Praeger, Publishers, 1965) and Peter Donaldson, *Machiavelli and Mystery of State* (Cambridge: Cambridge University Press, 1988).

20. S. H. Steinberg, *The 'Thirty Years War,' and the Conflict for European Hegemony 1600–1660*, 99.

21. S. H. Steinberg, *The 'Thirty Years War,' and the Conflict for European Hegemony 1600–1660*, 99–100.

22. Richard Bonney, *The Thirty Years' War, 1618–1648*, 68.

23. S. H. Steinberg, *The 'Thirty Years War,' and the Conflict for European Hegemony 1600–1660*, 96.

Index